CW01467412

First published 2024 by Macmillan Children's Books,
an imprint of Pan Macmillan,
The Smithson, 6 Briset Street, London EC1M 5NR
EU representative: The Liffey Trust Centre,
117–126 Sheriff Street Upper, Dublin 1, D01 YC43
Associated companies throughout the world.
www.panmacmillan.com

In association with Alison Green Books,
an imprint of Scholastic Children's Books,
1 London Bridge, London SE1 9BG

ISBN: 978-1-0350-0494-2

Written by Amanda Li
Text copyright © Julia Donaldson 2024
Illustrations copyright © Axel Scheffler 2024

The permission acknowledgements on page 169 constitute an extension of this copyright page.

Moral rights asserted.
All rights reserved. No part of this publication may be reproduced, stored in a retrieval system,
or transmitted, in any form or by any means (electronic, mechanical, photocopying,
recording or otherwise), without the prior written permission of the publisher.

Pan Macmillan does not have any control over, or any responsibility for,
any author or third party websites referred to in or on this book.

Designer: Liz Adcock
Editor: Teresa Gale
Special thanks to: Amy Boxshall, Molly Butler-Crewe, Sophie Cashell,
Chris Inns, Nicole Pearson, Alyx Price and Lizzie Yeates.

1 3 5 7 9 8 6 4 2

A CIP catalogue record for this book is available from the British Library

Printed in China

FSC
www.fsc.org
MIX
Paper | Supporting
responsible forestry
FSC® C116313

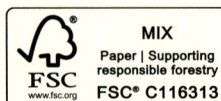

The Amazing World of

Julia Donaldson and Axel Scheffler

Written by Amanda Li

MACMILLAN CHILDREN'S BOOKS

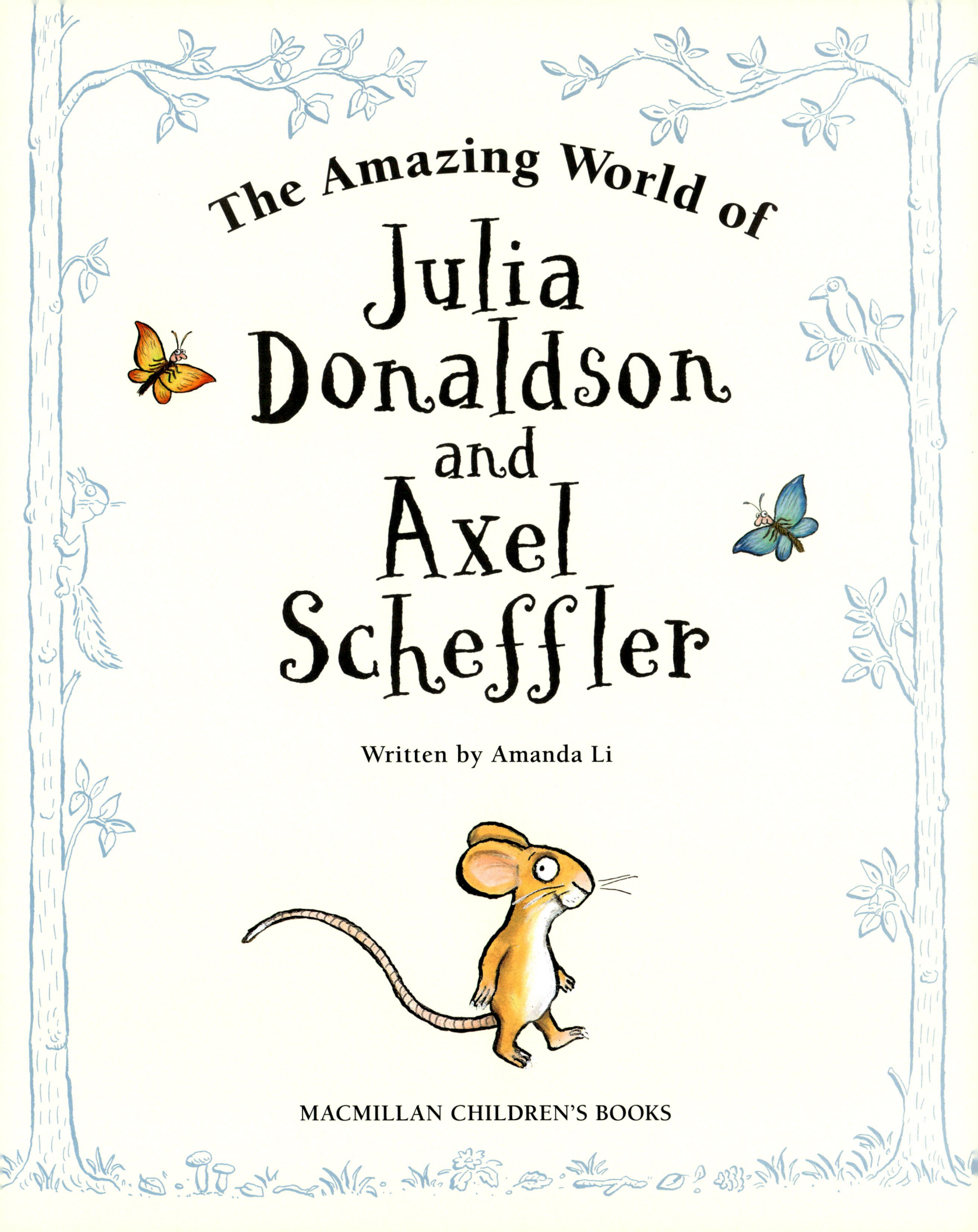

Contents

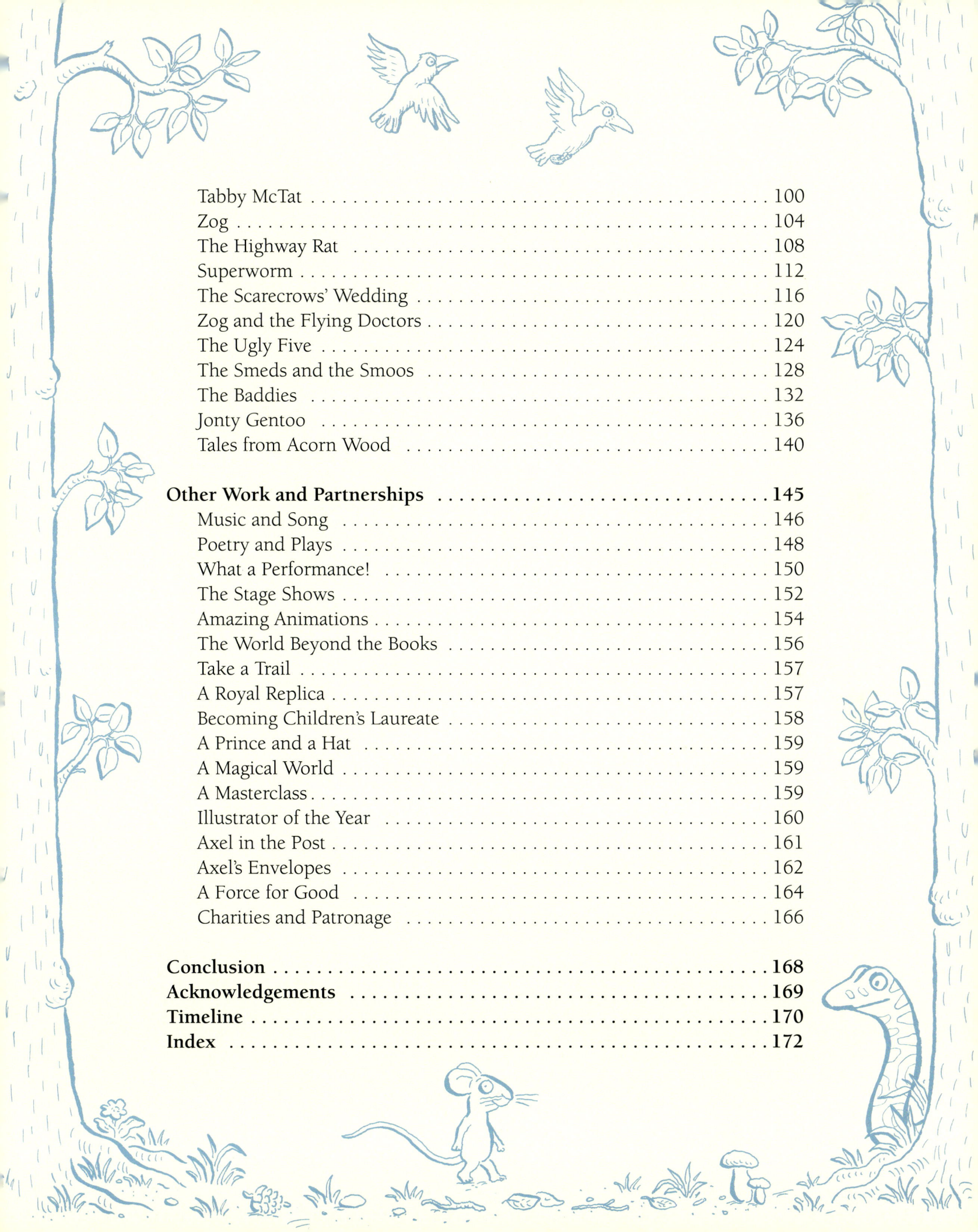

Foreword

How fortunate I am to be asked to write the foreword to this wonderful behind-the-scenes celebration of the creators of these beloved stories and illustrations. Welcome to *The Amazing World of Julia Donaldson and Axel Scheffler*.

And what a world it is . . .

I have long admired the combined magic of Julia and Axel's work, having read their stories innumerable times to all five of my children. I treasure the memory of early-evening bedtimes, in particular reading my two favourites, *The Snail and The Whale* and *The Highway Rat*, relishing the rhythm and rhyme. Julia writes in such a deceptively simple and beautifully economical way, with never a wasted word. Her prose flows from the page and is a delight to read aloud. It lends itself so easily to emerging – as another writer once put it – trippingly off the tongue . . . Axel's vibrantly immersive signature illustrations are the perfect accompaniment, a vivid and distinct realisation of Julia's imagined worlds.

Why have I been asked to provide the introduction? Well, long ago and faraway in 2009, I was lucky enough to be asked to perform the voice of the Snake for the Magic Light Pictures animated adaptation of *The Gruffalo*. I have since performed voices for all their interpretations of Julia and Axel's work, sometimes as narrator, sometimes, as with *Room on the Broom*, the small but nonetheless pivotal role of the Cat – just an occasional miaow.

No matter the size of the role or the number of words, being involved in Julia and Axel's world is a great honour and pleasure. I couldn't be happier to have stumbled into this association with these two remarkable creative minds in a series of animated films that will be cherished and enjoyed long after I've left the stage.

This beautiful compendium is a book to be enjoyed today and then passed down to future generations. How lucky they are as they take their first steps into *The Amazing World of Julia Donaldson and Axel Scheffler*. I sincerely hope you and your family will derive as much pleasure from Julia and Axel's enchanting tales as we have. Enjoy!

Rob Brydon, 2024

My partnership with Axel Scheffler has been one of the most enriching things in my life. It's funny to think that we didn't actually meet till after our first book together, *A Squash and a Squeeze*, was published. We were at a publisher's party and I asked him what sort of books he most liked to illustrate. His answer, "Fairy Tales", stuck in my mind and probably helped me to create the Gruffalo who, though not a fairy, is somehow from that world.

We have now created twenty picture books together, as well as ten of the younger Acorn Wood lift-the-flap series, and every time Axel manages to surprise and delight me with his illustrations to my stories. His pictures are always so faithful to my words, and then there are the witty extra details – a bug biting a dragon's tail in *Zog*, a princess looking glum because the frog she's married hasn't turned into a prince in *The Smartest Giant in Town*, or a Gruffalo fish mingling with all the real ones in *Tiddler*.

It's also lovely to have Axel on the stage when I'm performing at a book festival. As well as entertaining the audience with his drawings, he's also a pretty good actor, his star roles being the Owl in *The Gruffalo* and the wise old man in *A Squash and a Squeeze*. Thanks to Axel, I have also learned to act a lot of the roles in German, as we've done a number of German tours together.

I don't actually watch Axel at work, which is something most people perhaps don't realise. So this book has given me, as well as all the other readers, the chance to see a huge number of his initial sketches for the characters and settings of the stories. It's also given me the opportunity to put into words how I go about writing each one. I hope you'll enjoy it, and that perhaps some of the children learning about us might become the authors or illustrators of the future.

Julia Donaldson

2024

My life would have been very different if, in 1992, a publisher hadn't been looking for an illustrator to create the pictures for *A Squash and a Squeeze*. A friend suggested me and that was the start of my incredible journey with Julia. Several years later, the same friend became the children's book publisher at Macmillan, and she realised the great potential of *The Gruffalo* after I shared with her the text that Julia had written and sent to me. I had little idea that a monster success was in our hands, which forged our partnership to this day.

Now I meet adults who grew up with *The Gruffalo* and it not only shows me my age but also the incredible longevity and universal appeal of the monster and the mouse. I've been so lucky to have this partnership with Julia, who has written not just one masterpiece, but has done it again and again. Contrary to what many people assume, we work completely separately and the unity of text and images only happens on the pages, with the help of the editor and the designer. Sometimes it seems like a miracle to me that it has worked so well.

As Julia is solely in charge of the stories, I never really know what the next one is about, but I'm glad that there has been such a variety of themes, from baddie rats, snails and aliens to sticks and worms. It's almost as if Julia is trying to challenge me . . . what next?

I like the way that Julia's stories have subtle messages to make the world a slightly better place: they show us how to help creatures that are in trouble or to be open and loving to beings that are different from us. Although, nobody should, of course, follow the Highway Rat's example and steal chocolates and buns from others!

Over the years, Julia and I became friends and have done many signings, events and theatrical performances together. Like many illustrators, I'm not somebody who likes to perform in front of people, but prefer to be sitting at my desk drawing. Little did I know that I would be lured into acting on stage and asked to take on some extremely challenging roles, like a beetle who fell in a well and even a melting snowman.

I've learned a lot about Julia's work reading this book and hope you will find it interesting to have a peek into our way of making picture books. Maybe some of you will be inspired to become creative yourselves.

Axel Schuffler

2024

Beginnings

Discover where it all began with this look at
the early lives and careers of Julia Donaldson and
Axel Scheffler before they became the nation's
favourite picture-book partnership.

Julia Donaldson's Early Life

Julia Catherine Shields was born in September 1948, in London. She grew up in a Victorian house with three floors. Julia lived with her parents and her sister Mary on the ground floor. Her aunt and uncle – Beta and Chris – lived on the first floor, and her grandmother was up at the top.

Julia and her granny sitting on the wall outside their home in London.

Julia and her family at their home in Hampstead.
Back left–right: Julia's father, Auntie Mary.
Middle left–right: Julia's mother, Auntie Beta.
Front left–right: Mary, a friend, Julia.

The house was near a big, wild grassy area called Hampstead Heath, where Julia and Mary spent a lot of time climbing the trees, watching the squirrels and feeding the ducks on the ponds. Julia's love of nature started here: with the help of the book *I-Spy Wild Flowers*, she got to know the names of all the flowers she found on the heath. Sometimes a fair would come and there was the excitement of the swing boats, the ghost train and candyfloss.

The sisters had busy lives, with piano and ballet lessons and being in the Brownies, and later the Girl Guides. They loved playing board games, especially Monopoly, with Auntie Beta and Uncle Chris upstairs. They also enjoyed making up shows to entertain their family and friends, which is when Julia wrote her first songs.

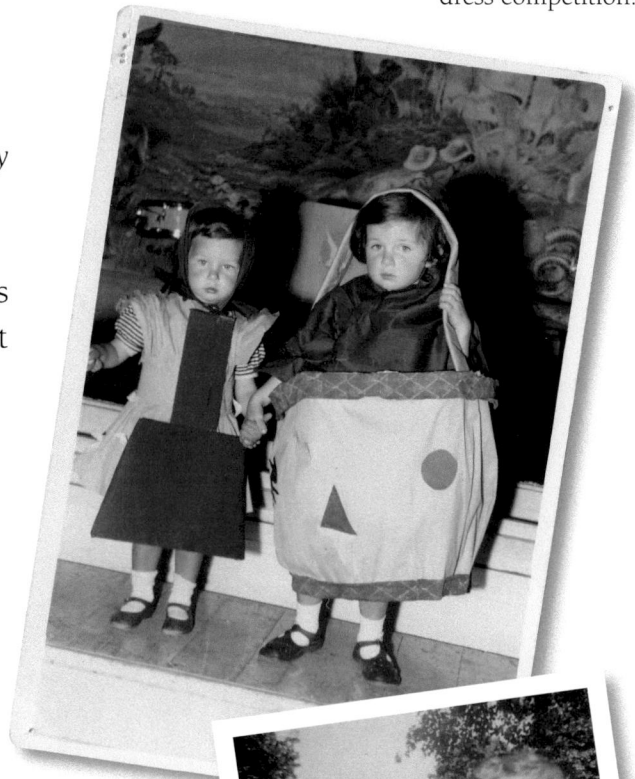

Julia and her sister Mary dressed up as a bucket and spade for a fancy dress competition.

Julia and Mary on Hampstead Heath.

Julia and Mary also had a cat called Geoffrey. When they were younger, they believed that Geoffrey was really a prince in disguise, and hoped he might marry one of them one day!

Teenage Mary with Geoffrey the cat.

15

A Love of Reading

Julia's parents often read stories to her and Mary. One of Julia's favourites was *Leo, the Adventures of a Lion Cub* by Peter, which included a description of some imaginary creatures called the Chintergongs. They looked a bit like elephants, but with long, stripy legs, and they sang:

"We are the Chintergongs!
Kapoo, Kapish, the Chintergongs!
Sing as we prance along
HARROOOH!"

But, best of all, Julia loved a book her father gave her for her fifth birthday. It was called *The Book of a Thousand Poems*. Julia learned a lot of the poems and began making up some of her own. She decided that she wanted to become a poet one day.

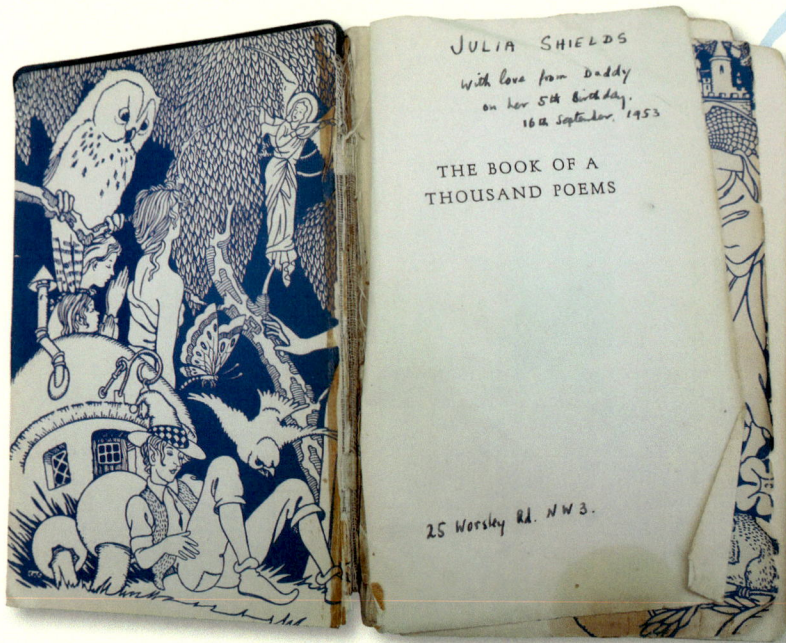

Julia Says . . .

"I read the poems, recited them, learned them and then started making up some of my own."

Julia has kept this book all her life.

Sometimes Julia and Mary went upstairs to watch their granny's television. Their favourite programme was *The Adventures of Sir Lancelot*, about the Knights of the Round Table.

Granny also introduced them to the poet and artist Edward Lear. She read them his nonsense alphabets and limericks (they always demanded the one about the old man with a beard full of nesting birds), as well as poems like 'The Owl and the Pussy-cat'.

An original wood-engraving illustration of the Owl and the Pussy-cat, 1871.

Lear's verses had a strong influence on Julia's own writing. In 2014, she wrote a poem called 'The Further Adventures of the Owl and the Pussy-cat', which was made into a book with illustrations by Charlotte Voake (another Lear fan). This time, instead of going to sea 'in a beautiful pea-green boat', the two animals set off from the Land of the Bong Tree in 'a beautiful blue balloon' and meet some of Lear's other characters, like the Pobble Who Has No Toes.

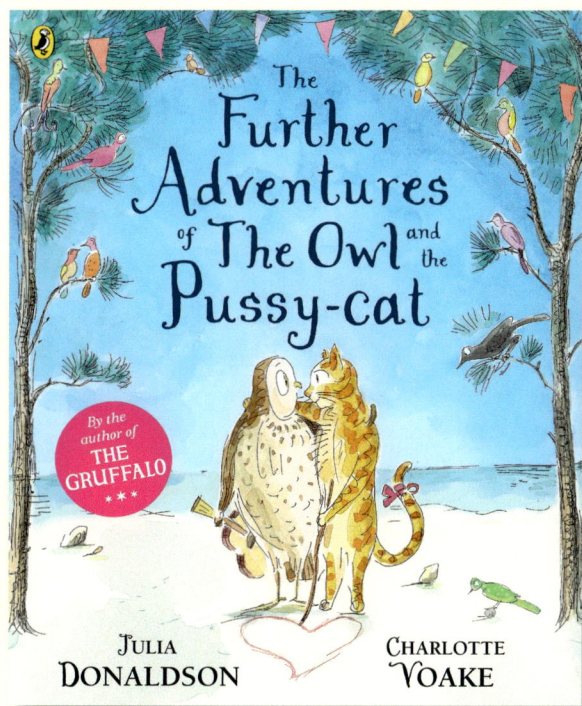

The Further Adventures of the Owl and the Pussy-cat (Puffin, 2017).

Julia Says . . .

"Edward Lear taught me that there can be a lyrical beauty in nonsense."

From Page to Stage

Julia always enjoyed reading. She visited the library and second-hand bookshops as a child, discovering authors such as Noel Streatfeild who created the theatrical world of *Ballet Shoes*, and Mary Norton who wrote *The Borrowers*. She especially enjoyed Richmal Crompton's William books. There are thirty-eight books about eleven-year-old William who is always in trouble, and Julia collected lots of them.

When Julia wasn't reading, she sometimes made up her own plays, stories and songs. Her granny used to slit open big, brown envelopes for Julia and Mary to write and draw on. Julia remembers writing a story about a wizard who lost his tail and another one about a rabbit with orange ears.

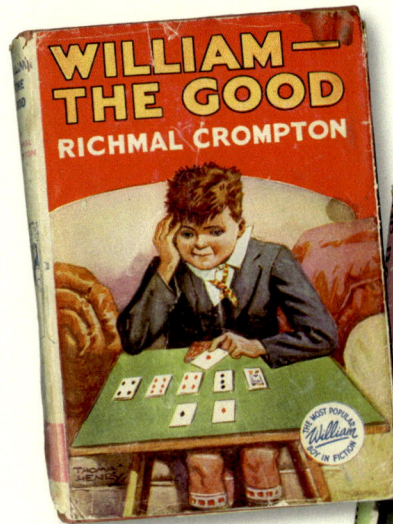

Julia still has her original copies of some of her childhood favourites.

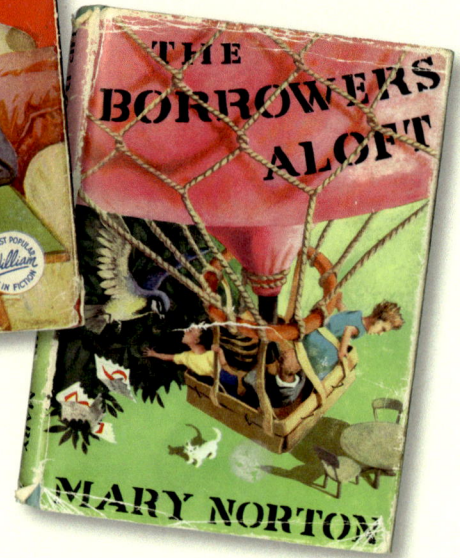

Julia Says . . .

"I wrote a short play based on Little Red Riding Hood. *My mother played the wolf and my father was the woodcutter – but he couldn't stop laughing while saying his lines!"*

Where the fields were white whith snow
Where I walked a week ago,
Now I see that there is grass,
Wild flowers smile as I pass.

SPRING

One of Julia's first poems.

Julia's childhood home was filled with music and song. Her mother sang in a choir and her father enjoyed playing his cello. As well as learning the piano, the two sisters joined the Children's Opera Group for the chance to sing and act. This was when Julia began to fall in love with theatre.

When Julia was twelve, she got a part as an understudy for the fairies in Shakespeare's *A Midsummer Night's Dream* at the Old Vic Theatre in London. This was a thrilling experience as she was able to watch the actors – including a young Dame Judi Dench – from the wings of the stage. If one of the fairies was ill and couldn't perform, Julia got the chance to act their part. She changed her mind about being a poet: now she wanted to become an actress.

A copy of the programme for the 1960 production of *A Midsummer Night's Dream.*

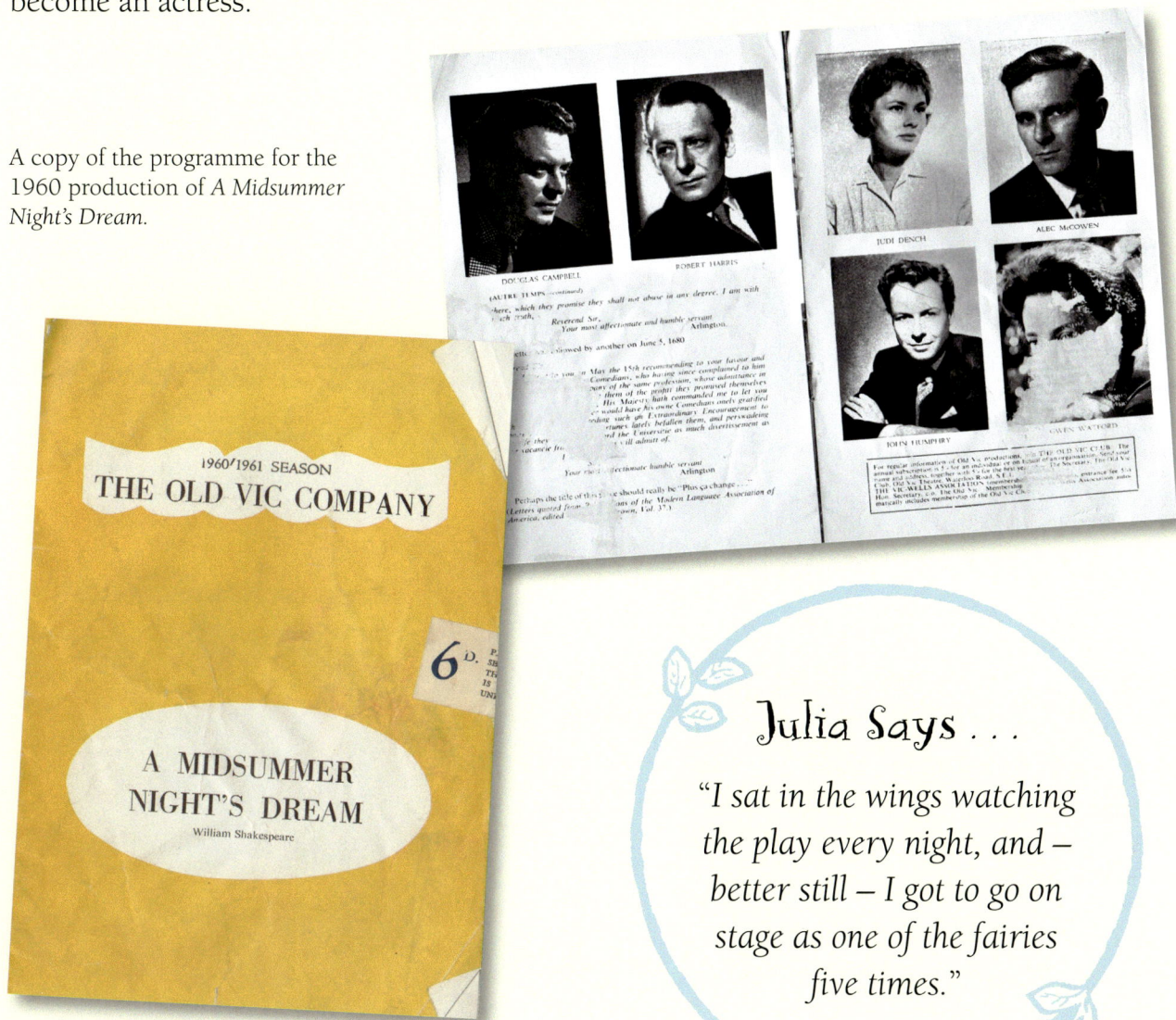

Julia Says . . .

"I sat in the wings watching the play every night, and – better still – I got to go on stage as one of the fairies five times."

University and Beyond

With acting in mind, Julia went to the University of Bristol to study Drama and French. Alongside her studies, she took part in student plays, acting roles including a French maid, a middle-aged housewife and a tree!

It was at Bristol that Julia met a guitar-playing medical student called Malcolm. When Julia and a friend were studying in Paris as part of their French course, Malcolm hitchhiked to join them and the three of them went busking together – singing pop songs to people in cafes and collecting money in a big straw hat. One day, the hat blew into the River Seine and Malcolm dived in to rescue it.

Julia and Malcolm performing together at university.

Years later, Axel Scheffler did this sketch of Julia and Malcolm busking in Paris.

Julia and Malcolm busking in Italy.

Back in Bristol, Julia and Malcolm – who were now going out together – started performing at local events. Julia would often create a song for the occasion. She wrote one about teeth for a dentists' dinner and another about eggs for an Easter parade. When they went abroad, she sometimes wrote songs in the different languages; there was a French busking song, and the Italian 'Spaghetti Song' all about pasta. This was later published as a children's book in Italy, with illustrations by Nila Aye.

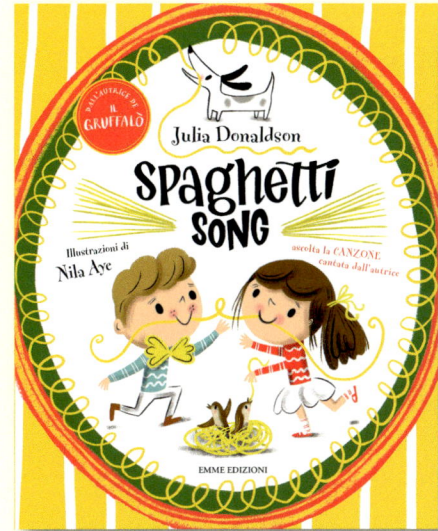

The Spaghetti Song, published by Italian publisher, Edizioni El, 2020.

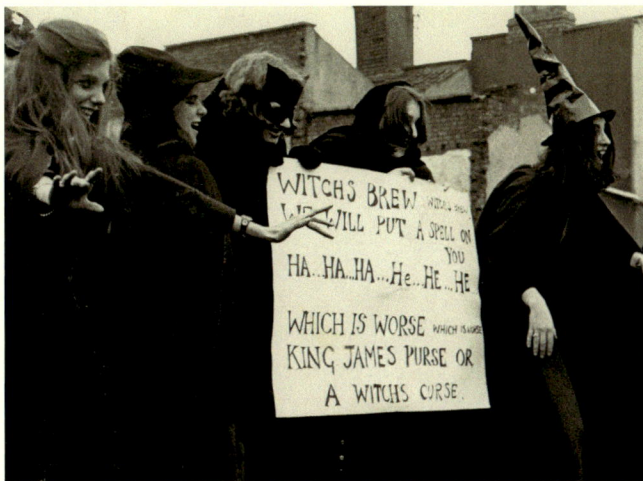

The couple joined the Bristol Street Theatre, a group that made up plays and performed them outdoors, encouraging children in the audiences to join in. This later had a big influence on Julia's own shows, in which she often invites children on stage.

Julia, second from left, performing with Bristol Street Theatre – it was lots of fun, but also a bit chaotic!

In 1972, Julia and Malcolm were married, and Julia wrote some special songs for their wedding. There was a proposal song and others for the bridesmaids, best man and ushers to sing.

Julia and Malcolm travelling from the church to the reception in the rag-and-bone man's horse and cart.

Although Julia still loved acting, a career on the stage would mean long periods apart from Malcolm, so after university she began doing some other jobs – working for a publisher, a local radio station and teaching English in a secondary school. But she continued to write songs and when she sent a recording to BBC Children's Television, they asked her to write some more for well-known programmes like *Play School* and *Play Away*. Julia found herself writing about all sorts of different things, including photography, prehistoric fish and Sherlock Holmes!

While still in her twenties, Julia wrote a musical called *King Grunt's Cake*. It was performed by a group of actors, including herself as the kitchen cat and Malcolm who acted both King Grunt and a Morris-dancing farmer.

Julia as Lola the kitchen cat in her musical, *King Grunt's Cake*.

A later musical, *Pirate on the Pier*, showcased Julia as a scheming fortune-teller and Malcolm as a forgetful treasure-hunting pirate. Malcolm has always loved singing and acting with Julia, somehow fitting it all in with his successful career as a doctor.

An original poster from Julia's musical.

22

They started performing at local folk clubs, which was an opportunity for Julia to write more 'grown-up' songs. Under the folk club label, they released an album of some of these called *First Fourteen*. A second album, *Second Fourteen*, was to follow many years later.

By this stage, Julia and Malcolm had a son called Hamish. Two more boys, Alastair and Jerry, were to follow, so life grew very busy. However, Julia continued to write songs and plays – many of which she put away in a drawer for later – as well as singing and acting whenever she could. Then, out of the blue, when she turned forty, there came a call from a publisher who wanted to turn the words of one of her songs, 'A Squash and a Squeeze', into a picture book.

This was the beginning of Julia's hugely successful career in children's books and her long-standing creative partnership with Axel Scheffler. With her love of music, acting and writing, it is really no surprise that she became a children's author and performer, who is now famous for her stories, songs and entertaining shows.

Julia Says . . .

"Although I now write more books than songs, I don't feel I've deserted music, as writing a rhyming story is very much like writing the words of a song."

Axel Scheffler's Early Life

Axel Scheffler was born in December 1957 in Hamburg, Germany. A middle child, Axel lived with his family, including his older sister, younger brother and their pet canary, in a house in the suburbs of the city.

Axel spent his spare time playing football, watching television and sometimes going to the cinema with his family. He has happy memories of watching all the big Disney movies of the time, animated cartoon films like *Bambi* and *Snow White and the Seven Dwarfs*. Unsurprisingly, given his job now, he also loved drawing and colouring books.

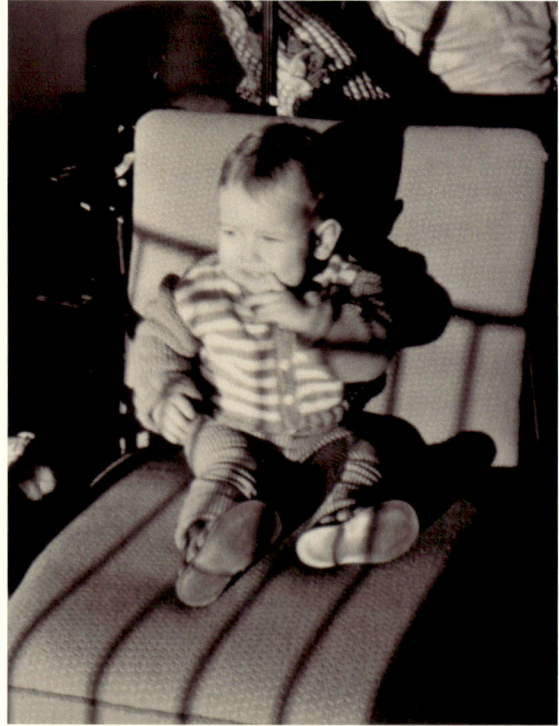

Axel as a toddler, 1959.

Axel Says . . .

"I sometimes daydreamed of being a famous footballer like all little boys, and I liked animals and TV – and dinosaurs, of course!"

Axel on his first day of school. He is holding a cardboard cone filled with sweets, stationery and toys – a German tradition.

As a young child, Axel loved looking at comics and he always looked forward to the treat of choosing a new one. He knew that if he went to the dentist without a fuss, a trip to the newsagent for a new comic would be his reward!

One of Axel's favourite comic characters was a Danish character called Petzi, a little bear who travelled the world on a boat with his animal friends.

Axel Says . . .

"Petzi was featured in comic strips without speech bubbles, but with the words underneath. I loved to read the adventures of little animals going around the world."

Petzi by Carla and Vilhelm Hansen, published by Carlsen Verlag, Germany.

Axel also loved Disney's Mickey Mouse and Donald Duck cartoons, which were very popular with children at the time. Another cartoon favourite was a character called Snoopy, a thoughtful beagle who is owned by a boy called Charlie Brown. Snoopy communicated in thought bubbles and often lay on his kennel daydreaming of being something more exciting – like a pilot or an author!

Although Axel didn't own many books as a child, he always enjoyed trips to the library. He also had a copy of *Grimm's Fairy Tales*, which his mother read to him. These tales include classics such as *Cinderella*, *Rapunzel* and *Hansel and Gretel*. Axel didn't know then that he would one day be illustrating his very own books.

A Budding Artist

A self-portrait, aged 8.

Axel concentrating hard on his drawing, aged 8.

A snowy drawing by a young Axel.

Axel at the zoo!

Axel Says . . .

"I started drawing as a child. I think most illustrators do start when they are children and just keep doing it."

From a young age, Axel enjoyed drawing and colouring. As a teenager, he won his first art prize when he drew a cow for a competition run by the Milka chocolate company. Their logo was a cow – and Axel's prize was also a cow! Not a real one, but a cuddly lilac soft toy that he still owns.

An Art teacher called Mr Eggers saw that Axel had talent and inspired him in his artistic studies. It went so well that when Axel completed his final exams, he got top marks in Art.

Axel painting, aged 14.

As a teenager, Axel discovered the work of Tomi Ungerer, a French artist and writer who created many books for children and adults during his long career, as well as posters, sculptures and collages. Axel was drawn to his slightly dark humour and his eye for detail. He also liked illustrators and cartoonists such as Jean-Jacques Sempé and Edward Gorey, both of whom had their own distinctive style and humour. Much later, when Axel started illustration himself, these early influences inspired his own work.

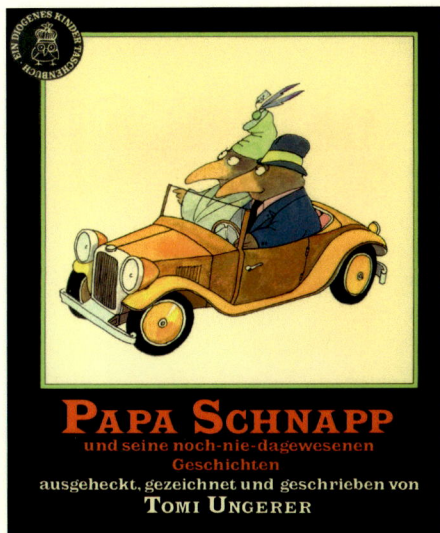

Papa Schnapp by Tomi Ungerer, published by Diogenes Verlag, 1987.

Axel Says . . .

"I discovered satirical and cartoon drawing in my late teens and I would look at books with all these artists' drawings – I really loved them."

27

University and Art School

When Axel left school, he wasn't sure exactly what he wanted to do. He won a place to study History of Art at the University of Hamburg. However, he soon discovered that it was easy to get lost in the system with so many students at lectures and in large classes. It wasn't right for Axel, so he decided to leave university without graduating.

In 1980, Axel completed sixteen months of National Service, which was compulsory for all men in Germany at the time. Instead of serving in the military, he did civilian service and worked in the community, helping people with mental ill-health. It was during this time that Axel went on a trip to England, which inspired a new direction for his studies and career. During the holidays, he visited a friend who was studying Ceramics at Bath Academy of Art. Axel liked the idea of studying here, so he applied to do a degree in Visual Communications – and he got in!

Axel moved to England in 1982, at the age of 25, and began his new course. It covered a whole range of skills, from drawing and graphic design to print-making and photography.

There were lots and lots of sheep in the Wiltshire countryside.

Axel did a lot of observational drawing – sketching from things he could see in real life – during the three-year course, which was a very good grounding for a future illustrator.

Luckily for him, the art campus was based at Corsham Court, a lovely old manor house surrounded by countryside and gardens with peacocks. During his time at Bath Academy of Art, Axel kept sketchbooks as part of the course. His student sketchbooks are full of the sheep and peacocks he observed on the campus grounds.

Axel Says . . .

"I liked the idea of living and working in another country, and Britain's membership of the European Economic Community at the time made this easy to do."

Sketches of the peacocks Axel saw at Corsham Court.

A sketch of the busy high street in Corsham, 1985.

29

In 1984, while Axel was a student in Bath, he had the opportunity to go on an exchange trip to New York. He attended Cooper Union Art College for three months and made the most of his exciting new surroundings. His sketchbooks from this time are full of his lively drawings of the people and places around him.

Left and below: some photographs Axel took during his stay in New York.

New York etching, 1984.

Above: A sketch of a lady on a New York street.

Browsing at Doubleday's

Eichhörner Riverside ~~Drive~~ Park

Axel has always loved drawing squirrels and often includes them in his picture books.

At the end of his time at college, Axel graduated with a first-class degree and a big portfolio of drawings and paintings. Bath Academy had given him the chance to find out what he really wanted to do – and that was to become an illustrator.

McDonalds 1 Ave/6 St.

Axel Says . . .

"One of my tutors had suggested I go out and get work when I was still a student, so I already had printed work when I left art school, which was very helpful."

Drawings of people in New York, 1984.

THE AMAZING WORLD OF JULIA DONALDSON AND AXEL SCHEFFLER

After Graduation

London was the place to be: the buzzing city where all the big newspapers, magazines and publishers had offices. So that's where Axel went. He moved to a flat in Streatham Hill and began the job of taking his portfolio around to different companies. In those days before the internet, he had to make appointments by phone and visit their offices to show them what he could do.

These early magazine commissions from the 1980s show how Axel's illustration style has evolved over the years.

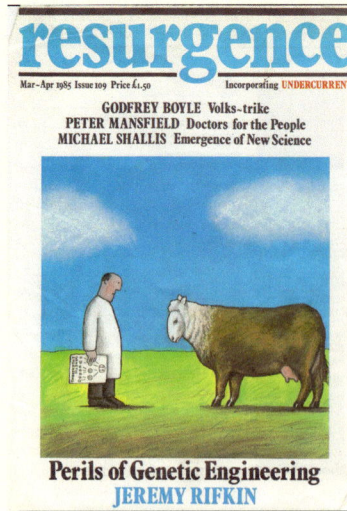

Axel succeeded in getting a steady stream of work. He did illustrations for magazines in both English and German, as well as for advertising companies. His tutors at art college had told him never to say no to a job, so Axel did everything he was offered and got lots of different experiences.

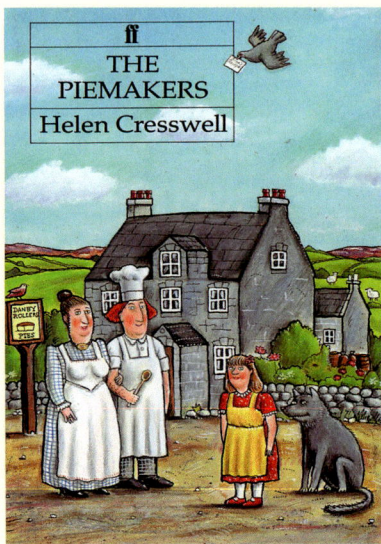

Axel knew that his illustrations would work well for children's books, so he began to visit different publishers with his art folder. He got his first book commission in 1988 from the publisher Faber and Faber. The book was called *The Piemakers*, by Helen Cresswell, and it told the story of a family who were asked to make a very special pie for the king – a pie that would feed 200 people!

The Piemakers, published by Faber and Faber, 1988.

32

Axel then started illustrating children's picture books, written in both English and German. One of the first German books he illustrated was a translation of an Edward Lear story, which is quite a coincidence because Edward Lear is one of Julia Donaldson's favourite poets. At this point, Axel and Julia didn't know each other – but that would soon change.

The first book Axel illustrated for his long-time German publisher, Beltz und Gelberg. The title is roughly translated as 'The Story of the Four Little Children Who Went Around the World'.

In 1992, Axel illustrated *You're a Hero, Daley B* by Jon Blake, a funny story about a rabbit who isn't sure what being a rabbit is all about. That same year he was asked to illustrate a story by an unknown author called Julia Donaldson. That story was *A Squash and a Squeeze* and was the start of their long creative partnership.

You're a Hero, Daley B, published by Walker Books UK, 1992.

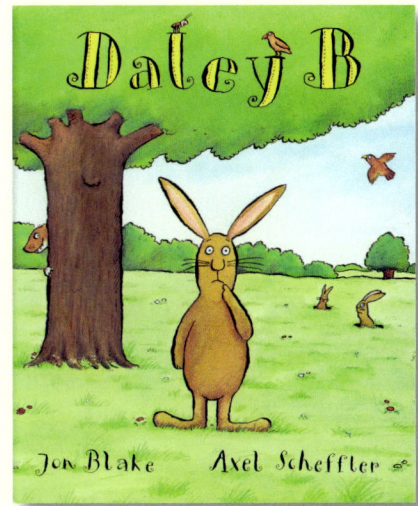

Axel hard at work in his studio.

Axel Scheffler is now one of the best-known and most successful children's book illustrators. He has lived in England for most of his life but has strong connections to his roots and spends a lot of time travelling to Germany and France, as well as many other countries around the world. Axel lives with his family in London and works in a studio at the top of the house, which is full of all his sketches and paintings for the many books he has illustrated over the years.

Coming Together

Take a look behind the scenes and learn all
about Julia Donaldson and Axel Scheffler's
first picture-book collaboration.

> "Wise old man, won't you help me, please?
> My house is a squash and a squeeze."

The Very First Book

Based on a traditional tale, this funny rhyming story began life as a song which Julia wrote for children's television. The little old lady is not happy – her house is too small, even for one. Whatever can she do? When the wise old man tells her to bring in a group of noisy, mischievous farm animals one by one, matters grow even worse . . .

The 1993 hardback cover of *A Squash and a Squeeze* published by Methuen Books.

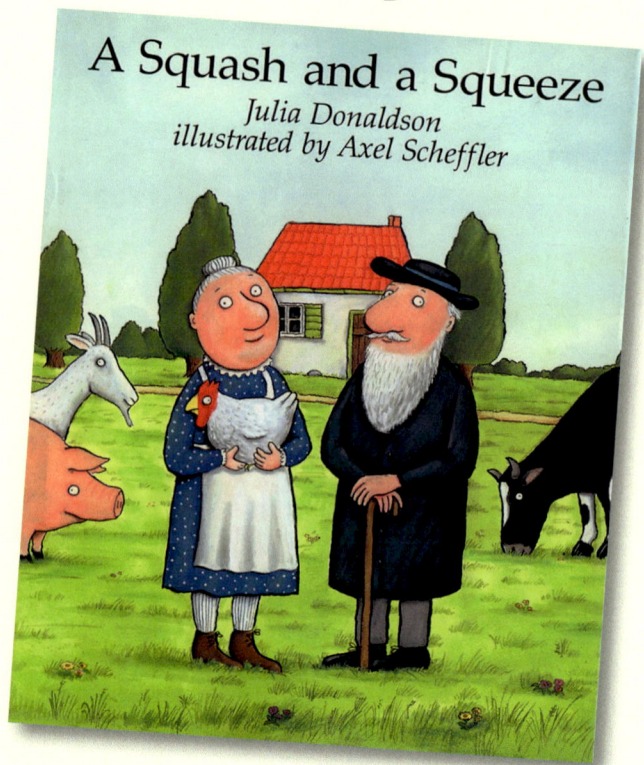

A Squash and a Squeeze was Julia Donaldson and Axel Scheffler's very first picture book together, but it wasn't always a book. The story started life as a song that Julia had written in 1975 for a BBC children's television programme. She had been asked to write some songs for a series called *Playboard,* in which a mole and a hedgehog visited the circus to watch a storytelling song being performed by shadow puppets. Julia supplied some songs based on Aesop's Fables, and then the producer suggested she might write one based on a traditional folk tale about an old lady whose house is too small. Julia agreed and set to work at once.

The song went down well; it was repeated several times and included on a BBC album, sung by the children's presenters Dame Floella Benjamin and Derek Griffiths. As luck would have it, years later, an editor at Methuen Children's Books who remembered the song from when her children were little, had the idea that the words could make a fantastic picture-book text and managed to track Julia down via the BBC. Julia was very surprised to receive a phone call from a publisher, as to her *A Squash and a Squeeze* was just a song which she had written a long time ago. But the offer of a book was incredibly exciting. In fact, it was so exciting that, when Julia put the phone down after speaking with the editor, she danced around the room – just like the little old lady at the end of the story!

Floella (bottom, centre) and Derek (top, third from right) with the presenters of *Play School*.

Julia Says . . .

"I remember being quite pleased with myself when I came up with the phrase 'a squash and a squeeze' because it rhymed with so many things: please, sneeze, fleas, agrees, knees and fiddle-de-dees."

It was soon clear that *A Squash and a Squeeze* worked brilliantly as a rhyming picture book. Now another very important person had to be found – the illustrator who could bring all of Julia's characters to life. Luckily, an up-and-coming young German artist, Axel Scheffler, loved the story and agreed to illustrate it. His humorous, quirky style was just right for conjuring up all the characters, from the wise old man to the riotous dancing cow.

Working with an illustrator was a first for Julia. She was both excited and a little nervous when she received the rough drawings for *A Squash and a Squeeze* and saw exactly how Axel had imagined her creations.

Julia Says . . .

"I loved Axel's pictures straight away. They added such humour to the story, telling it not just from the old lady's point of view but from that of the hen, the goat, the pig and the cow."

Axel did lots of rough drawings and sketches before he painted the final artwork. His initial sketches of the little old lady looked very different. She was very old, with lots of wrinkles and a big, pointy chin and nose. The editor thought she didn't look very friendly, so asked Axel to redraw her to give her a softer, cosier look.

Axel's frolicking farm animals were a perfect match for Julia's witty words and now it is hard to imagine the story being illustrated by anyone else.

In this early colour illustration, the little old lady has two hens – this would have been double the trouble!

A *Squash and a Squeeze* was published in 1993 and is now a much-loved children's classic that has sold millions of copies around the world in multiple formats, including special anniversary editions, audiobooks and activity books.

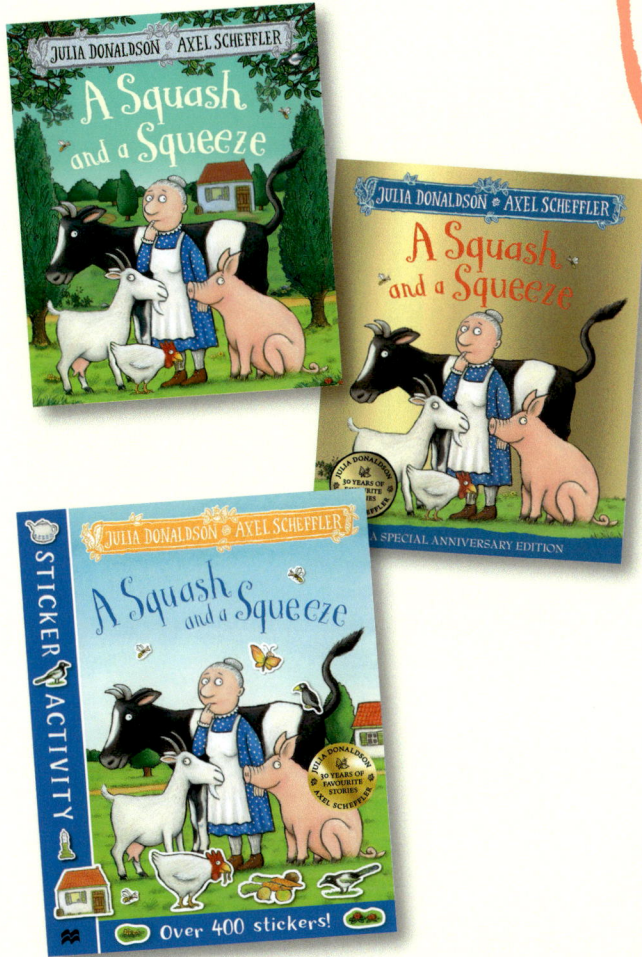

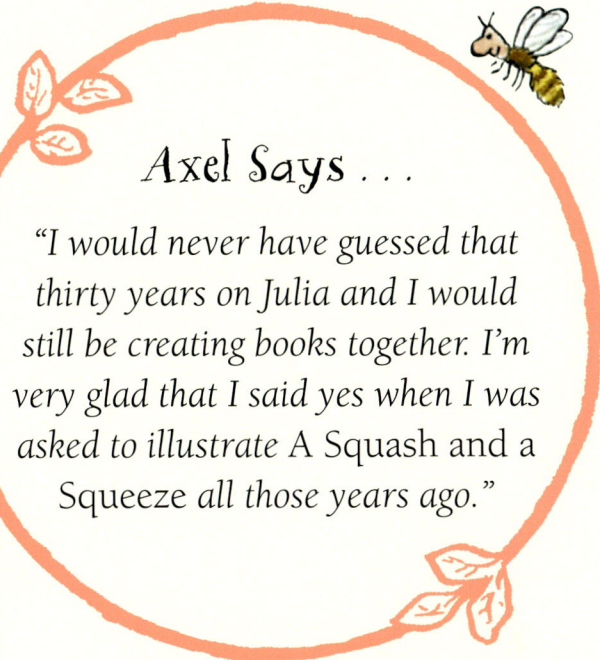

Axel Says . . .

"I would never have guessed that thirty years on Julia and I would still be creating books together. I'm very glad that I said yes when I was asked to illustrate A Squash and a Squeeze *all those years ago."*

It is also a story that lends itself to being acted out. When Julia started doing school visits, she would get the class in a circle to be the little old lady's house and then choose children to act the different animals. She still enjoys singing and acting the story as part of her live shows, usually with her husband Malcolm as a guitar-playing wise old man.

Top: new paperback edition, 2016.
Middle: 30th anniversary paperback edition, 2023.
Bottom: sticker activity book, 2018.
All published by Macmillan Children's Books.

The cast of Julia's show puppeteering the noisy animals.
Top row: Julia's husband Malcolm, actor Joanna Hutt.
Bottom row: Julia's sister Mary, Julia, actor James Huntingdon.

Axel did lots of sketches of the characters before starting the final artwork. Here is a page from his sketchbook.

Squash & squeeze

little old lady

The Perfect Pairing

Though they didn't know it at the time, *A Squash and a Squeeze* was just the start of Julia and Axel's long creative partnership. Since this first book, they have worked together in nearly the same way for every one of their books.

It is often thought that Julia and Axel must sit and create their books together, but that is not the case. Julia writes the story first and then Axel starts work on the illustrations. Axel often has no idea what Julia's next story will be about before he sees it.

Julia enjoying a walk on the Sussex Downs.

Julia's ideas can come from anywhere: childhood memories, everyday life, old folk tales – there are so many things that can inspire her. The hard part is developing an idea into a proper story with a beginning, middle and satisfying ending. This sometimes takes months or even years.

Julia does a lot of her thinking and planning when she is out walking in the countryside near her home, and she does a lot of her problem-solving in the bath!

Julia puzzling over a new story in the bath.

Once the story is clear in her head, Julia gets out a big notebook. In this, she writes out the storyline in a rough kind of way, finding phrases that please her and rhymes for some of the key words. She's always looking for a catchy line, like 'a squash and a squeeze' that can be repeated as a chorus, and when she finds the right words, they suggest the musical rhythm she needs to stick to.

Then comes the painstaking task of crafting the whole story. Julia usually shows a first draft to Malcolm, who reads it aloud. If he stumbles over any of the lines, Julia rewrites those bits to make them easier for a grown-up to read to a child. She keeps working on the text – usually for a couple of weeks – until she is completely happy with it, before sending it to her editor.

It is always a treat for Julia's editors to find a new story from her in their email inbox. Julia usually writes with one of her illustrators in mind, so when she hopes a text is for Axel, the editor then sends it to him to see whether he would like to illustrate it.

Julia Says . . .

"The hard part is turning a vague idea into a good storyline, so often the idea is in my head for months or even years before I start to write."

A selection of Julia's notebooks she writes her stories in. She often drafts more than one story in each notebook.

Once Axel has agreed to illustrate the new story, he works with the editor and the designer to discuss how each character will look. Axel often has to sketch lots of roughs to try to get a character or scene exactly right.

Sometimes Axel needs to find reference pictures to help him get the details right – like when drawing a wildebeest for *The Ugly Five* or a rainforest scene for *Monkey Puzzle*. Axel had great fun with the alien world in *The Smeds and the Smoos* as he could draw everything from his imagination.

Axel's early versions of the wildebeest from *The Ugly Five*.

Axel Says . . .

"When drawing real-world animals, they need to be recognisable, so I like to look at reference photos and then create my own version of the animal."

44

While Axel is working on the character development, Julia sits down with her editor to work out the pagination of the story: which lines of text should go on each page. Usually, picture books are thirty-two pages long, but the story takes up between twenty-four and thirty pages.

Julia and one of her editors, Alison Green, looking at some layouts together.

Axel busy painting an image of the Gruffalo.

Axel then starts on his rough sketches for the whole story – a mixture of full scenes and smaller images called vignettes. Often he will do multiple sketches for scenes to try out different ideas. Julia also gets to see the rough sketches and sits down with her editor to look at the layouts and discuss her feedback. Once everyone is happy, then Axel moves on to the final colour artwork using his watercolour paints, pen and ink, pencils and felt-tip pens.

One of Axel's favourite things to do is to add something extra to his scenes – a visual joke that the reader might not notice straight away. He came up with the idea of hiding an image of the Gruffalo in some of their other picture books, and children now have lots of fun searching for him.

Axel drew a gruffalo tractor, the 'Gruff-tor', in *The Scarecrows' Wedding*.

Into the
Deep Dark Wood

Take a walk through the deep dark wood and learn
all about the creation of Julia Donaldson and
Axel Scheffler's most famous character, the Gruffalo.

"A mouse took a stroll through the deep dark wood. A fox saw the mouse and the mouse looked good."

The Gruffalo is Born

The brave little mouse has captured the hearts of families around the world who have joined him for an adventure in the deep dark wood. When the quick-thinking mouse meets a fox, an owl and a snake, he must use his wits to get out of trouble. But to his surprise, the imaginary monster he creates to scare them turns out to be real and he finds himself face to face with . . . a gruffalo!

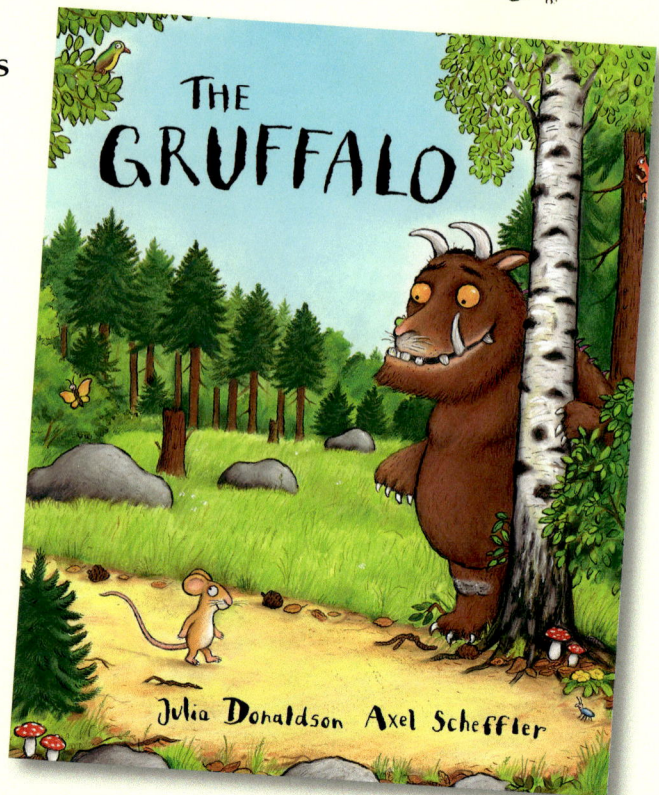

The 1999 hardback cover of *The Gruffalo*.

The Gruffalo is the title of the much-loved picture-book adventure that made Julia Donaldson and Axel Scheffler into household names. Since it was first published in 1999, it has become a modern children's classic and literary phenomenon, selling millions of copies all around the world in over a hundred languages.

48

But, just how did this story about a cunning little mouse with a big imagination make its way from the spark of an idea to one of the world's most famous children's books? Although Julia and Axel already had one publishing success with their first picture book together, *A Squash and a Squeeze*, it was another six years before *The Gruffalo* appeared on the shelves of bookshops and libraries.

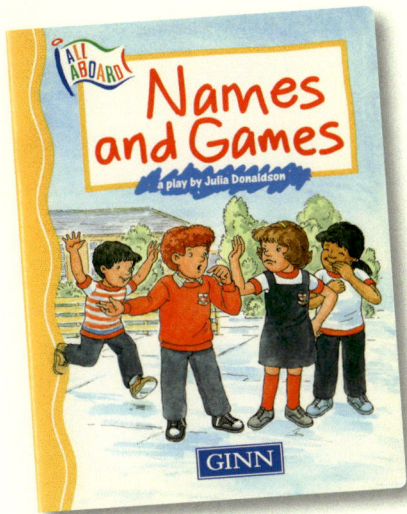

One of Julia's plays, *Names and Games*, published by Ginn in 1995.

During this time, Julia was busy looking after her family and writing in her spare time. The publication of *A Squash and a Squeeze* had given her the confidence to send to publishers the short plays she had written for children. This led to more work, writing stories and plays for schools.

It was while Julia was researching for one of her plays that the idea for *The Gruffalo* came to her. She had been asked to write some short plays for six children to act, based on traditional stories from around the world, and in her research she came across a tale about a clever child who tricks a hungry tiger and scares him away. There are many versions of this story, but the best-known is the Chinese folk tale 'The Fox That Borrows the Terror of a Tiger'. Julia thought it would be fun to make the main character in her play a mouse, and decided that the six parts would be a storyteller, the mouse, the tiger, and three other animals. Julia started to write the play, but then decided to keep the idea up her sleeve as it could make a good picture book. Now she's very glad she made that decision!

After mulling over her idea on and off for a year or more, Julia started to write. She decided that the three extra animals should be a fox, an owl and a snake, who all might like to eat a mouse. At first, Julia thought that she would have a tiger in the story, as in the original fable – but she couldn't think of anything that rhymed with 'tiger'. Instead, she thought up an imaginary beast – just the kind of monster that a bright little mouse might dream up to scare off his enemies.

Now, she needed to find a good name for this monster. She wanted it to rhyme with the mouse's words: 'Silly old Fox, doesn't he know?' and 'Oh help! Oh no!' so it needed to end with an 'o' sound. The name had to have three syllables, to fit the rhythm of the story, and Julia liked the idea that it could begin with a fierce-sounding 'gr'. Now she just needed the middle bit. Adding 'uffal' between the 'gr' and the 'o' made the creature's name rhyme with 'buffalo' which, as well as giving it the feel of a real animal, added quite a comical touch. And so, the Gruffalo was born!

A drawing by Axel Scheffler showing Julia at her desk, dreaming up the Gruffalo, except she wrote the story by hand rather than on a computer.

Writing the Story

Once Julia had worked out the storyline and started the actual writing, it took her about two weeks to get halfway through *The Gruffalo*. Then she found herself stuck as she couldn't think of a neat way of telling the second half in rhyme. She was about to give up on the whole idea when her son, Alastair, read what she had written so far. He loved it, and encouraged her to finish the story.

Julia busy working away on a new story.

Although picture books are quite short and often seem simple, writing one can be extremely difficult. Ideally, it should have an exciting story, a character you care about and also that special magic that makes you want to read it over and over again. Picture books don't always have to rhyme, but Julia, with her songwriting background, chose to write *The Gruffalo* in verse. This of course meant that when she was describing the Gruffalo she needed to use rhyming words, such as 'claws/jaws', 'toes/nose' and 'black/back' which helped create the monster's unique – and slightly scary – appearance!

51

Early drafts of *The Gruffalo*
from Julia's notebooks.

Drawing the Gruffalo

Once Julia had finished the story, she needed to find a publisher for it. The first publisher she approached sat on it for nearly a year, so Julia had the idea of sending the story to Axel Scheffler, even though she had only met him once – at a party following the publication of *A Squash and a Squeeze*. She sent the finished story by post to Axel in 1996, to see if he might want to illustrate it. Axel liked it immediately and, as it happens, his Macmillan publisher was coming to dinner that evening. He showed the story to her and she decided straight away that she wanted to publish it.

Once Axel started on the illustrations he had the task of bringing all of the animals in the deep, dark wood to life. Most importantly, what would the Gruffalo look like?

Axel had to use lots of imagination to bring the mysterious Gruffalo to life.

"He has terrible tusks, and terrible claws,
And terrible teeth in his terrible jaws . . ."

As a starting point, Axel focused on the Gruffalo's description in the story. His terrible tusks, teeth and claws, his orange eyes and purple prickles – and, of course, the poisonous wart at the end of his nose – were all there. But everything else was up to Axel. His first thought was that 'Gruffalo' sounded a bit like 'buffalo', so he drew the creature walking on all fours with buffalo-like horns.

53

Axel's Gruffalo evolved to walking on two legs . . .

. . . and then Axel started adding colour, too.

It took a little time for Axel to come up with the right look for the Gruffalo. The problem was that he had to be frightening enough to scare off the animals in the deep dark wood, but not too scary for small children. Axel eventually came up with a gruffalo that was a little bit scary, but also quite soft and cuddly – and now it's difficult to imagine him any other way.

This gruffalo is starting to look a lot more like the monster we know and love!

It would have been much easier to draw the Gruffalo if he'd come to Axel's studio.

A Mouse with Clothes?

Once the character of the Gruffalo had come to life, it was time for Axel to focus on the other animals in the story. The mouse also began life on all fours before Axel redrew him walking on two legs like the Gruffalo.

Then he had another thought – perhaps the animals should be wearing clothes? He experimented with different outfits, putting the mouse in a striped shirt and shorts, then in lederhosen.

A selection of Axel's early sketches of the characters from the deep dark wood.

However, Julia and her editor both thought differently: they felt that as the animals were in their natural surroundings there was no need for clothes. Eventually, Axel agreed and was secretly quite relieved as he didn't have to work out how to dress some of the trickier animals, such as the snake!

Mouse

Axel Says . . .

"I originally thought all the animals would be wearing clothes, as they often do in picture books."

Drawing the Deep Dark Wood

When the question of clothes was decided, Axel worked on developing the full pictures for the story. He made a rough mock-up of the whole book, with all the text laid out along with his sketches showing what the illustrations would be for each page. Once the layout of the pages was agreed with Julia Donaldson and the publisher, Axel started on the final colour artwork.

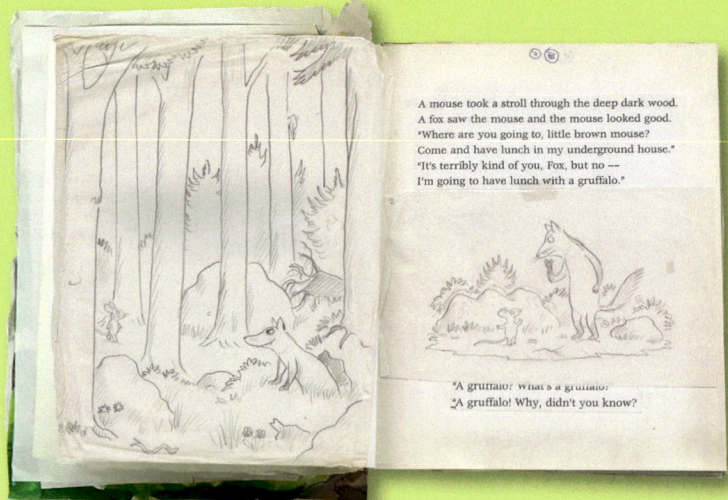

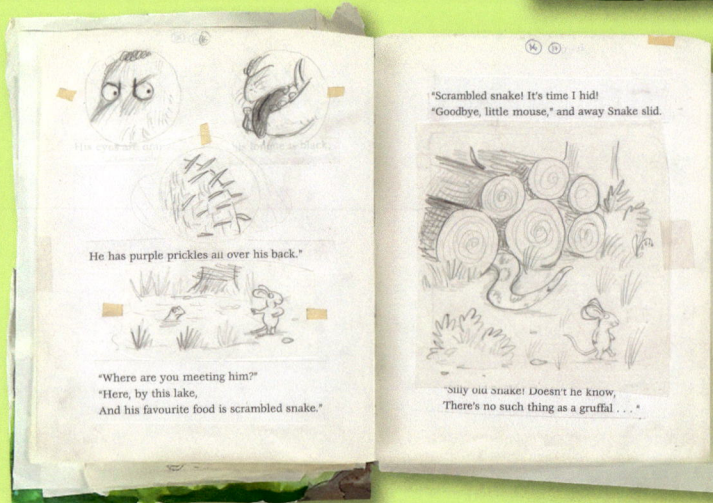

Spreads from Axel's mock-up of *The Gruffalo*.

Creating the Cover

Sometimes an illustrator draws many versions of a book cover before it looks right. Axel tried multiple different compositions for *The Gruffalo* before doing the artwork for the final cover design.

Can you see any similarities between the final cover design (directly below) and Axel's early sketches?

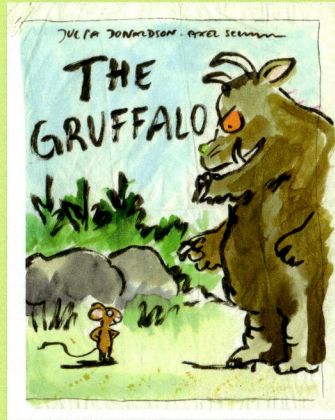

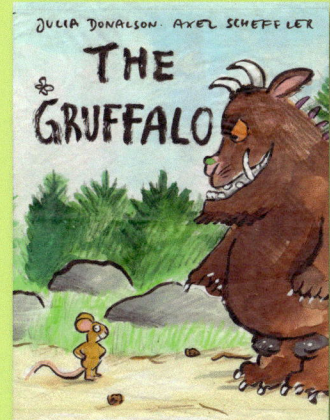

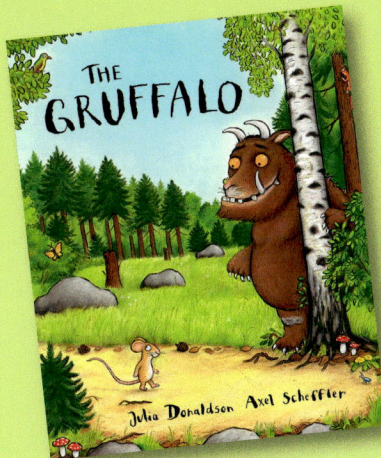

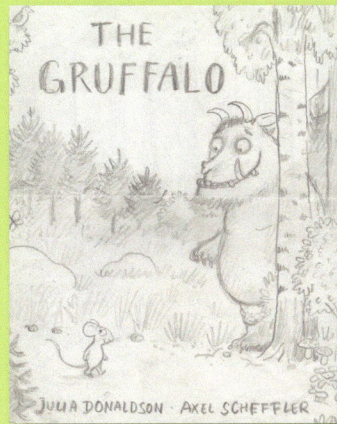

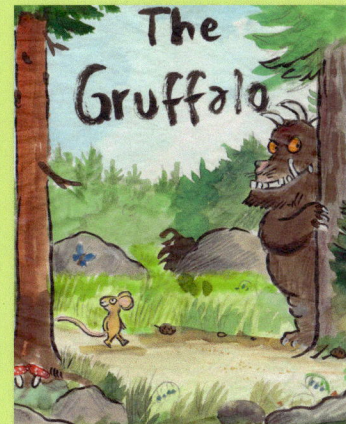

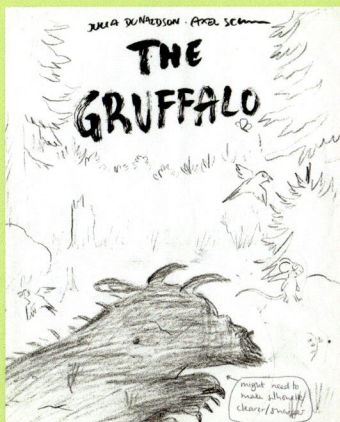

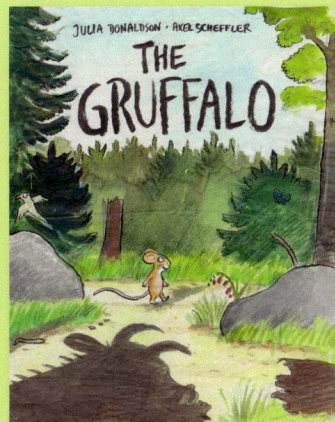

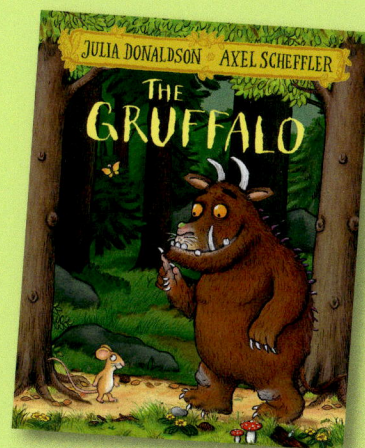

In 2016, a new cover design (above) was created, with a special foil banner.

A mouse took a stroll through the deep dark wood
A fox saw the mouse and the mouse looked good
"Where are you going to dinner
etc ... etc ...

Axel also found the deep dark wood a challenge to illustrate. After a few tries, he decided to go on a trip to a forest near Hamburg in Germany where he grew up, to take some photos for inspiration. But in the end, he didn't really use them. To this day Axel is still not completely happy with his woodland artwork.

Axel Says . . .

"Looking at it now, the forest is too light and bright. If I did it again today, I'd make the wood deeper and darker – more menacing."

A gruffalo
whati a gruff

An early version of the scene where the mouse first meets the fox.

Axel's final illustration
showing a very surprised
Mouse meeting the Gruffalo.
Axel used up all his green
and brown inks while
illustrating *The Gruffalo*.

A Monster Success

The Gruffalo was published in March 1999 and was an immediate success with children and adults alike. In its first year, it won the Nestlé Smarties Book Prize for the best book for ages 0–5. Julia was delighted to accept this prize – wearing a Gruffalo hand puppet, of course! The Gruffalo became the UK's bestselling picture book in 2000 and won the Blue Peter 'Best Book to Read Aloud' Award in the same year.

You can read The Gruffalo *in over a hundred different languages and dialects. He has different names in different languages, too. Here are just a few of them . . .*

Το Γκρούφαλο
Greek

Mörkyli
Finnish

古飛樂
Mandarin

Yayazula
Turkish

גְרוּפוֹתִי
Hebrew

Gruffalon
Swedish

Y Gryffalo
Welsh

グラファロ
もりでいちばん
つよいのは?
Japanese

Il Gruffalò
Italian

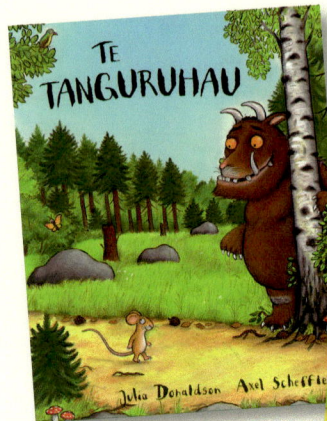

TE TANGURUHAU

Maori

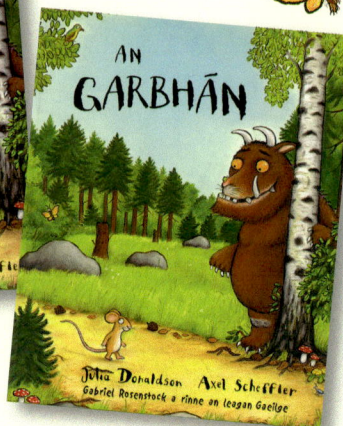

AN GARBHÁN

Irish

Bubulis un Bubulēns
Latvian

Der Grüffelo
German

ГРУФФАЛО
Russian

الْغَرْفول
Arabic

Grøflen
Danish

Greppikló
Icelandic

El Grúfalo
Spanish

O Grufalão
Portuguese

Die Goorgomgaai
Afrikaans

All of Julia and Axel's picture books are successful worldwide. However, *The Gruffalo* is extra special – a global phenomenon. The story can now be enjoyed in languages from Arabic and Cantonese to Vietnamese and Welsh, as well as dialects as diverse as Cornish, Kolsch and North Sami. There is even a version in Latin. It has also recently been translated into six Scottish dialects: Shetland, Dundonian, Orcadian, Doric, Glaswegian and Scots.

*"Whaur are ye aff tae, wee broon moose?
Will ye no hae yer denner in ma deep-doon hoose?"*

(Scots translation by James Robertson)

Translating any book from English to another language is a tricky task and *The Gruffalo* has certainly thrown up a few challenges for translators around the world. Because it is written in rhyme, there is the problem of finding the right rhyming words in a different language. In some countries you will find *The Gruffalo* text is still able to work in rhyme, thanks to clever translators, but in others, the story has to be written in prose.

It is also fun to see how different cultures have their own take on some of the British food mentioned in the story. In the Spanish version, 'scrambled snake' becomes 'snake tortilla', while in Scots, 'roasted fox' becomes 'hot tod stew'. In the first French translation, 'You'll taste good on a slice of bread' became 'You'll taste good on a bed of artichokes' ('Tu seras bon sur un lit d'artichauts')!

Beyond the Deep Dark Wood

Take a look inside the many wonderful worlds
of Julia Donaldson and Axel Scheffler's
picture books.

Since they first started working together over thirty years ago, Julia and Axel have created thirty books together, and counting.

Here they all are with their original cover designs.

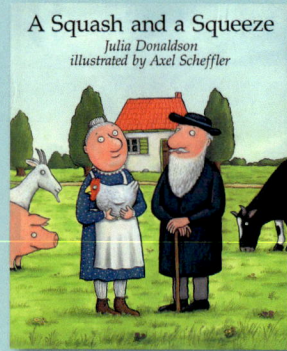

A Squash and a Squeeze
Julia Donaldson
illustrated by Axel Scheffler

1993,
Methuen Children's Books

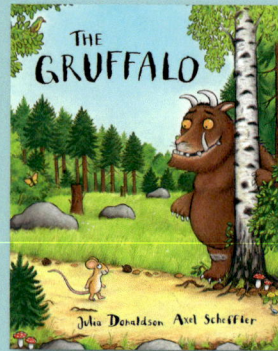

THE GRUFFALO
Julia Donaldson Axel Scheffler

1999,
Macmillan Children's Books

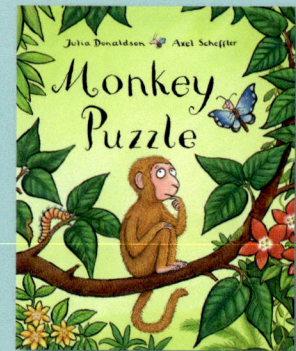

Julia Donaldson Axel Scheffler
Monkey Puzzle

2000,
Macmillan Children's Books

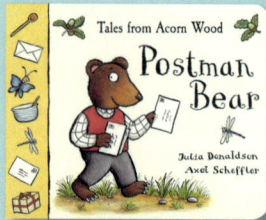

Tales from Acorn Wood
Postman Bear
Julia Donaldson
Axel Scheffler

2000,
Campbell Books

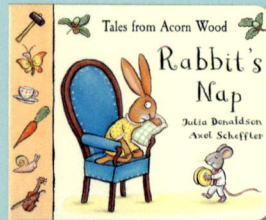

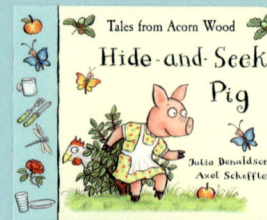

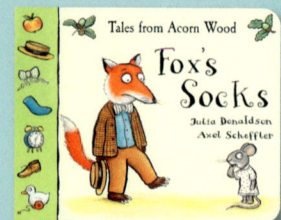

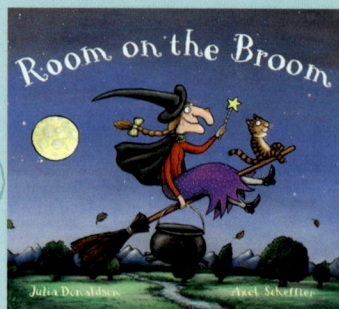

Tales from Acorn Wood
Rabbit's Nap
Julia Donaldson
Axel Scheffler

2000,
Campbell Books

Tales from Acorn Wood
Hide-and-Seek Pig
Julia Donaldson
Axel Scheffler

2000,
Campbell Books

Tales from Acorn Wood
Fox's Socks
Julia Donaldson
Axel Scheffler

2000,
Campbell Books

Room on the Broom
Julia Donaldson Axel Scheffler

2001,
Macmillan Children's Books

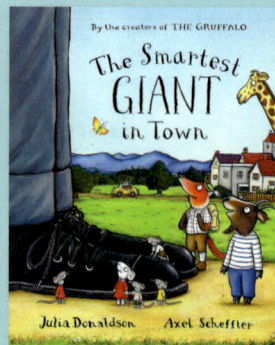

By the creators of THE GRUFFALO
The Smartest GIANT in Town
Julia Donaldson Axel Scheffler

2002,
Macmillan Children's Books

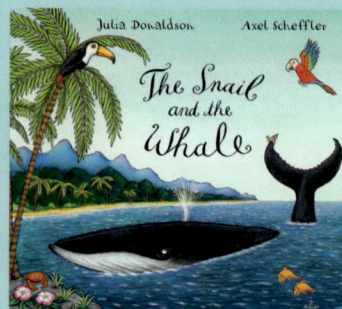

Julia Donaldson Axel Scheffler
The Snail and the Whale

2003,
Macmillan Children's Books

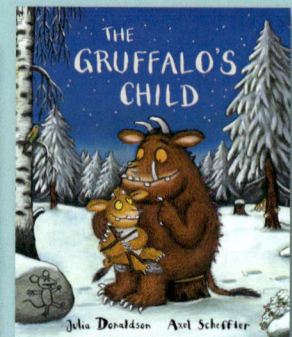

THE GRUFFALO'S CHILD
Julia Donaldson Axel Scheffler

2004,
Macmillan Children's Books

Julia Donaldson Axel Scheffler
Charlie Cook's Favourite Book

2005,
Macmillan Children's Books

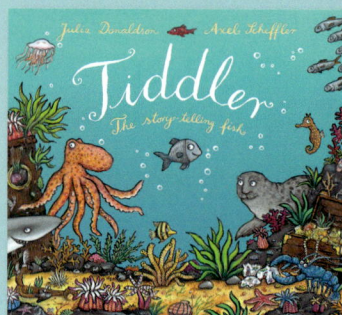

Julia Donaldson Axel Scheffler
Tiddler
The story-telling fish

2007,
Alison Green Books

STICK MAN
JULIA DONALDSON AXEL SCHEFFLER

2008,
Alison Green Books

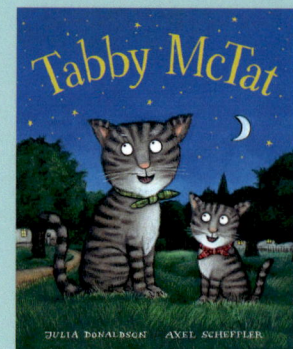

Tabby McTat
JULIA DONALDSON AXEL SCHEFFLER

2009,
Alison Green Books

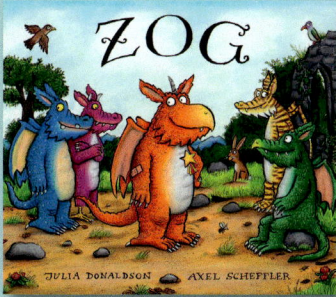

2010,
Alison Green Books

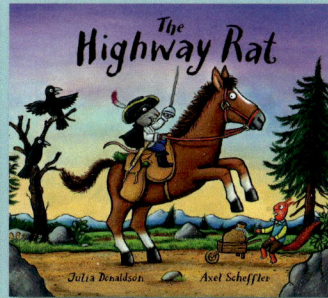

2011,
Alison Green Books

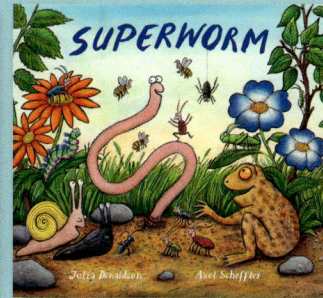

2012,
Alison Green Books

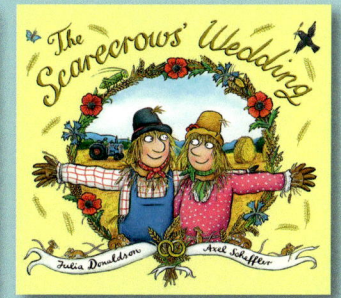

2014,
Alison Green Books

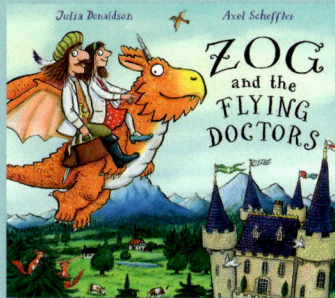

2016,
Alison Green Books

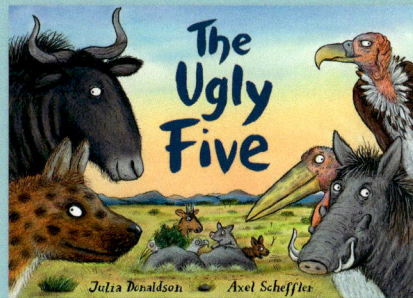

2018,
Alison Green Books

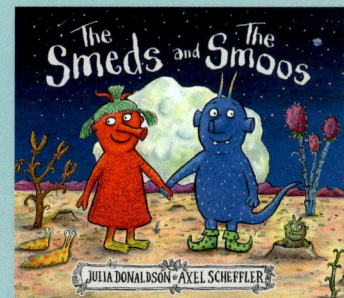

2019,
Alison Green Books

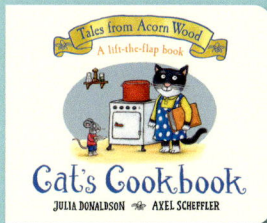

2021,
Macmillan Children's Books

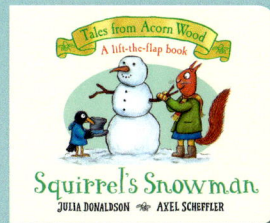

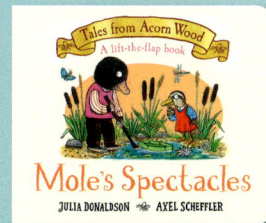

2021,
Macmillan Children's Books

2022,
Macmillan Children's Books

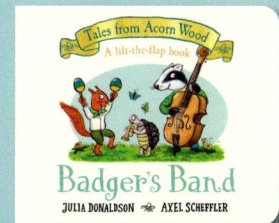

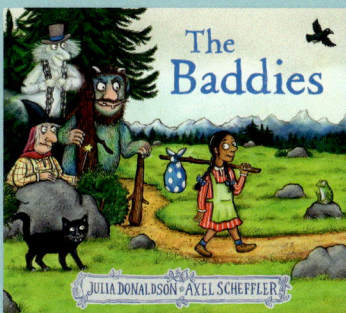

2022,
Macmillan Children's Books

2022,
Alison Green Books

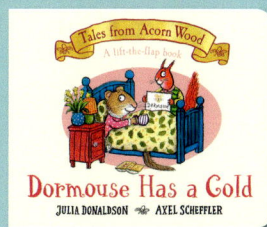

2023,
Macmillan Children's Books

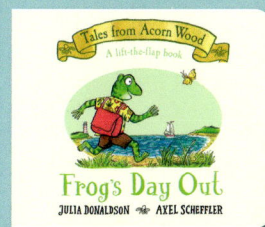

2024,
Macmillan Children's Books

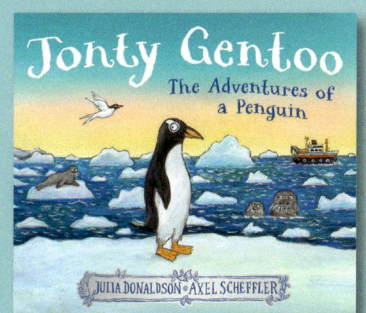

2024,
Alison Green Books

"Hush, little monkey, don't you cry.
I'll help you find her," said Butterfly.

Monkey Puzzle

Monkey Puzzle tells the story of a little monkey who has lost his mum. Kindly Butterfly is keen to help, but they don't seem to be having much luck as Butterfly keeps leading them to the wrong jungle animals. Finally, the little monkey explains that his mum looks just like him – much to the butterfly's surprise because, of course, none of her baby caterpillars look like her – and he finds his way home for a big hug.

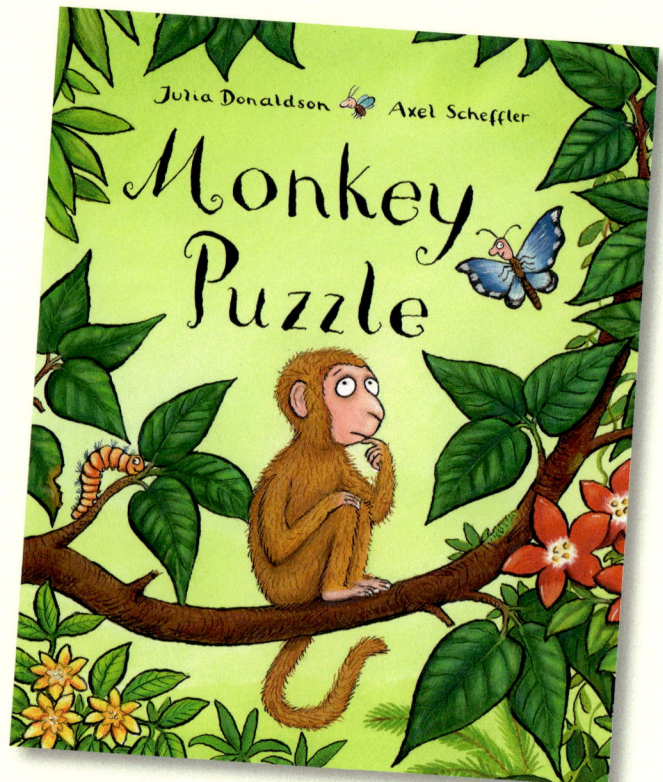

The original 2000 hardback cover of *Monkey Puzzle*.

Like *The Gruffalo*, this story is set in a forest full of animals. However, the little monkey's home in the vibrant, colourful rainforest is very different to the deep dark wood of the Gruffalo.

Julia's original story went through a few changes over time, although the little monkey was always the star of the show. An early version included a child swinging from a vine, but it was later decided that all the characters should be rainforest animals. The result was an amazing array of animals: a snake, a spider, a parrot, a frog, a bat – even an elephant. And, of course, the funny, helpful butterfly who presents us with the surprise twist in the tale. No one can draw butterflies like Axel!

The inspiration for the title came from the name of the monkey puzzle tree; there was one in Julia's neighbour's garden. The publisher did suggest a few alternatives, such as 'Where's My Mum?', but in the end decided to go with Julia's original idea.

The publisher accepted *Monkey Puzzle* before Axel had started working on *The Gruffalo* and briefly considered choosing a different illustrator for *Monkey Puzzle*. But this idea was soon abandoned as it became obvious that Axel would be perfect for both books. It was worth the wait. *Monkey Puzzle* was published a year after *The Gruffalo* and has now been in print for more than twenty years. It is one of Julia and Axel's most popular books.

Julia Says . . .

"I can't imagine that anyone other than Axel could have given such character and humour to the animals that the butterfly mistakes for the monkey's mum."

The rainforest setting and colourful creatures of *Monkey Puzzle* were exciting new subject matter for Axel. Although he and the editor researched many of the animals and plants, Axel used his imagination and creativity to give everything in the rainforest his unique quirky look.

One challenge for Axel was working out the scale of each creature in comparison to the others. He took a few artistic liberties with the size of the animals, especially the spider and the elephant, in order to fit them in alongside the monkey and the butterfly – but it worked out perfectly in the end.

Axel experimented with lots of different monkeys and butterflies in his sketchbook.

Axel Says . . .

"I enjoyed drawing all the different kinds of animals and the jungle vegetation – which I kind of made up (unlike the artist Henri Rousseau, who went to the botanical gardens when he did his jungle painting)."

To help him see how the artwork would look spread across the pages, Axel made himself a tiny book before he started the final illustrations.

Axel also did more than one version of some of the final artwork for the book. Here is an alternative version of the scene where the little monkey and Butterfly meet the frog.

"I am a dog, as keen as can be.
Is there room on the broom for a dog like me?"

Room on the Broom

The witch and her cat are zooming through the sky on their broomstick when – oh no! – the wind blows away the witch's hat. Luckily, help is at hand and, one by one, a dog, bird and frog join the ride after picking up the witch's lost belongings. But when the frog jumps for joy, the broomstick snaps and the witch, all on her own, finds herself pursued by a hungry dragon who fancies 'witch and chips' for his tea. The witch's animal friends had better think fast to come up with a plan to escape!

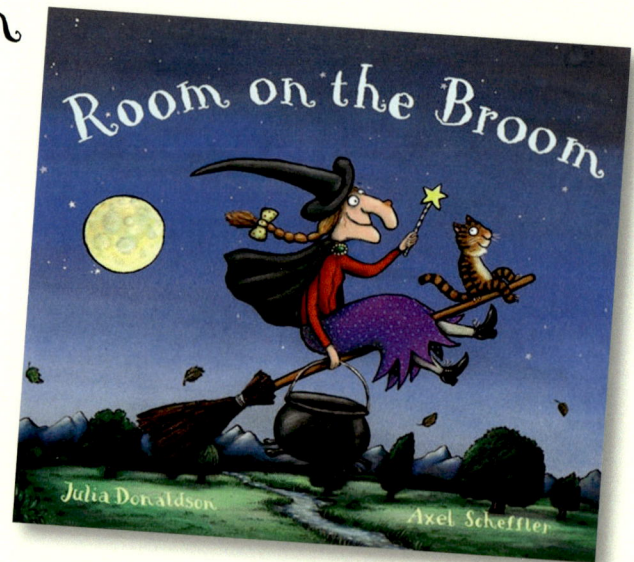

The original 2001 hardback cover of *Room on the Broom*.

Witches in children's stories usually have a cat but Julia wanted her witch to have some extra passengers on her broomstick.

Julia Says . . .

"I asked myself, 'Why do witches always have a cat? Why not some other animals as well?'"

Julia needed to find a reason for the other animals to climb onto the broomstick. She decided that the witch could drop various possessions which would then be found by the dog, the bird and the frog. But what would happen with so many passengers on the broomstick? It would snap, of course, but the witch could eventually make a potion and spell to create a 'truly magnificent broom'.

There wasn't a dragon in Julia's first draft of the story, but then she thought she needed to add some more excitement. So she dreamed up the scary dragon, and her tale of friendship and bravery began to come together.

There were other influences, too. Julia later realised that she had a traditional German tale called 'The Musicians of Bremen' in the back of her mind. This story is about four animals who frighten off a band of robbers by climbing on each other's backs and making a terrible noise. Julia's animals also climb on top of each other, creating a monster to scare off the hungry dragon.

The inspiration for the character of the witch came from Julia herself. When she was a child, she was always dropping and losing things just like the witch in *Room on the Broom*. Even now, Julia often leaves a trail of lost things behind her!

The mysterious mud monster scares off the hungry dragon.

73

Julia was quite surprised when she saw Axel's first sketches of the witch. She had imagined her to be young and untidy-looking, but Axel's witch was neatly dressed and older, and her long nose had a wart on it – a bit like the Gruffalo's one, but not green. Of course, now it's hard to imagine her any other way.

The witch didn't become any younger or neater, but she did go through some other changes, including to her clothes. She started off wearing a jacket instead of a cape, and her hat was much smaller. At one point, she wore a green top and tights instead of red.

The one thing Axel struggled with was painting the stormy skies in the background, with their muddy browns and greys. He painted the sky again and again to get it just right. There were many times he wished the witch could have gone flying on a sunny day instead! In the end, Axel's skies looked moody and atmospheric, perfect for the stormy day that causes the witch's things to blow away.

Axel Says . . .

"I was close to despair doing the stormy skies. The first picture I did about nine times. The paints just wouldn't do what I wanted them to do!"

Two early versions of the witch and her cat flying on their broomstick through the storm. The sky isn't the only thing that has changed – Axel also played around with different colours for the witch's clothes, and even her cat.

"My tie is a scarf for a cold giraffe . . .

. . . but look me up and down – I'm the smartest giant in town!"

The Smartest Giant in Town

George feels comfortable in his comfy old gown and sandals, but when he gets fed up with being the scruffiest giant in town, he decides to buy himself a smart new outfit. On his way home, he meets several animals in trouble and gives away his clothes to help them. As a result, he grows colder and colder, especially when he gives away his belt and his trousers fall down. He goes back to the shop to buy some replacement clothes, but – oh no – it's closed. Luckily, his comfy old clothes are waiting for him outside – perfect for the kindest giant in town.

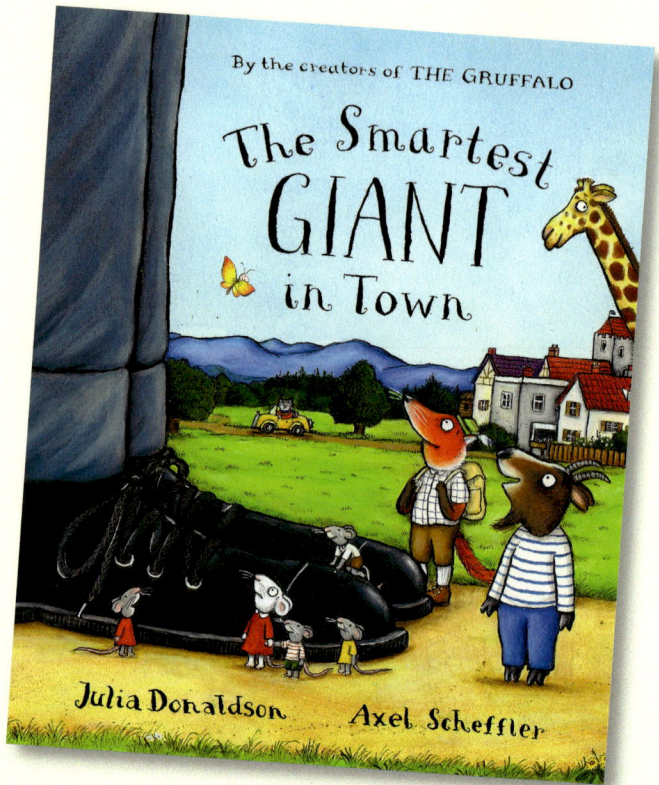

The original 2002 hardback cover of *The Smartest Giant in Town*.

Julia likes to vary her stories, and if she has a bad or scary character in one book – like the dragon in *Room on the Broom* – she prefers to avoid doing so in the next one. So instead of writing about the sort of scary giant we usually find in fairy tales, she created one who was kind to everyone. This helped her with the ending to the story, in which the animals give a gift and card to George to thank him for helping them.

One of Julia's inspirations for this story was a favourite childhood book, *The Borrowers* by Mary Norton. It is about a family of tiny people who live hidden under the floorboards and 'borrow' useful objects from the people in the house above them to furnish their own home. For instance, a cotton reel becomes their table, and a letter is used as paper for their wall.

Julia Says . . .

"I was fascinated by how familiar, everyday objects had completely different uses. For example, the Borrowers had a stamp on the wall as a picture and used a chess piece as a statue."

Julia found this idea of scale very appealing and she had fun deciding what George's clothes could become for the different animals in her story. One of her favourite illustrations is of George's sock being used as a sleeping bag by the fox.

The Smartest Giant in Town is the only one of Julia's books with Axel which isn't totally in rhyme. Julia did originally write a rhyming version in which the giant was called Ethelred! But then she had the idea of giving him a song which would get longer and longer as he gave away each item of clothing. The song, with its chorus, 'Look me up and down, I'm the smartest giant in town', just didn't fit into the rhyming framework so she started all over again and wrote the story in prose.

77

Whenever Axel is asked to name his favourite of his picture books with Julia, *The Smartest Giant in Town* is always near the top of his list. He loved being free to create a complete fantasy world of animal and human characters.

Axel Says . . .

"I enjoyed drawing the backgrounds and all the little details, as well as mixing animals, people and giants."

In Axel's first sketch for the opening scene, George the giant originally wore trousers and a coat.

In this later sketch, Axel gave George his comfy old gown and sandals.

Axel added lots of extra background characters to this first scene as his sketches developed, including two more giants, a lady pushing a pram and even a cat fishing in the fountain.

Julia loved spotting all the funny little details Axel included in the illustrations, such as the rabbit puzzling over a 'Missing Giraffe' poster when the giraffe is on the pavement beside him!

Not all of the illustrations were quite as Julia had imagined. When she wrote about George's new socks having diamonds up the sides, she had imagined a diamond pattern, but in his first few sketches Axel drew George with knee breeches and long socks decorated with real diamonds. These looked very smart indeed, but to go with those old-fashioned clothes, George's tie would have needed to be a cravat, rather than a more modern long tie which could become a scarf for the giraffe in the story. So Axel obligingly drew the lovely cosy socks that appear in the final book.

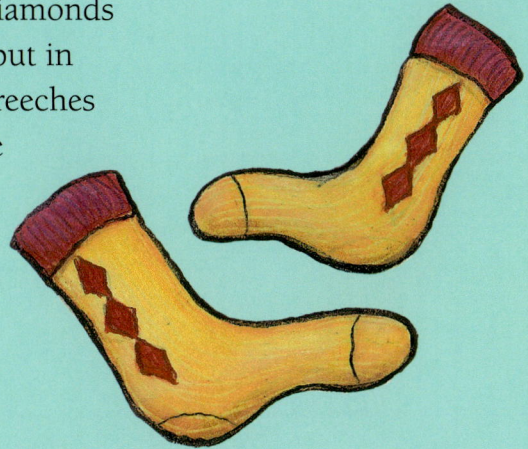

The cover of *The Smartest Giant in Town* also went through several changes before everyone agreed on it.

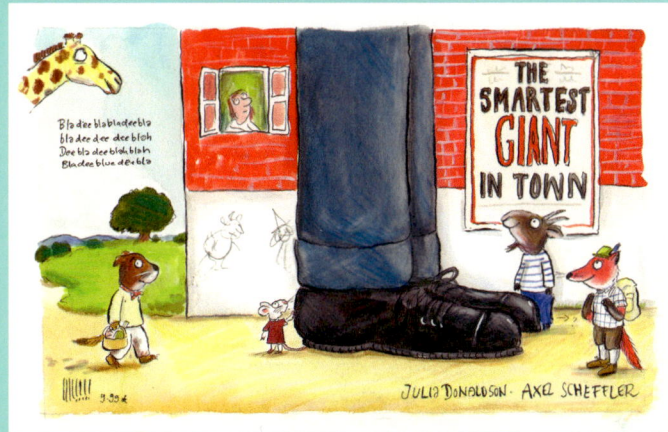

Axel's first design showed a poster displayed on a red brick wall.

He was later asked to draw another more scenic version which showed the town in the background. This became the final cover design.

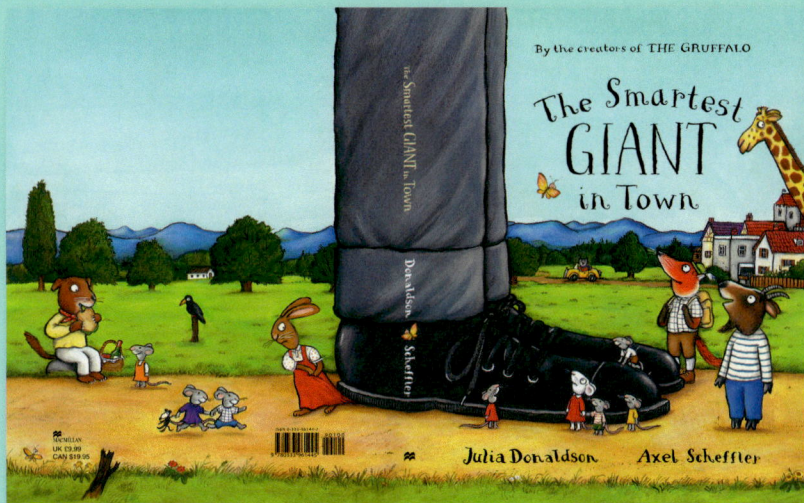

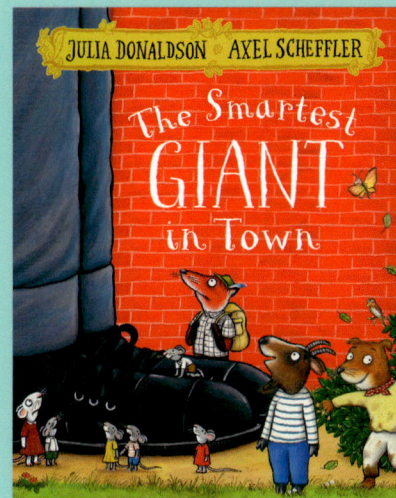

However, Axel's first idea didn't go to waste as a new edition of the story was published in 2016, complete with his original red brick wall.

"How I long to sail!" said the tiny snail.

The Snail and the Whale

A tiny sea snail longs to see the big, wide world, so she hitches a lift on the tail of a passing humpback whale. Together, they set off on an amazing adventure around the world, seeing wonderful things like icebergs, volcanoes and starry skies. But, one day, the whale swims too close to the shore and is beached in a bay. It's up to the tiny snail to come up with a plan big enough to save him.

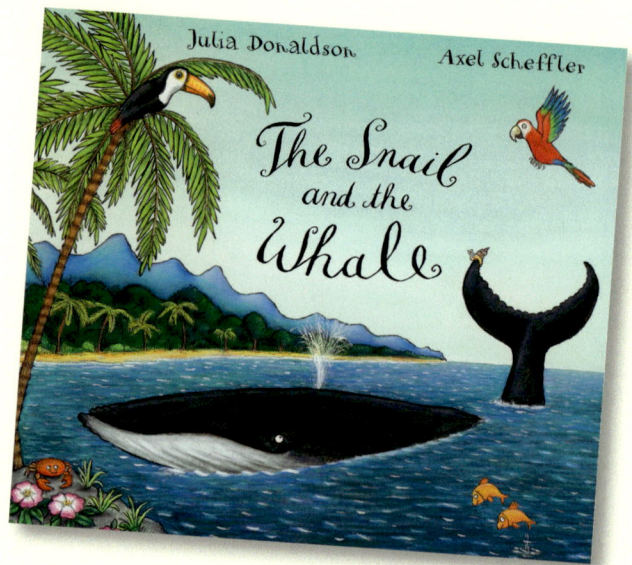

The original 2003 hardback cover of *The Snail and the Whale.*

Julia had recently written *The Smartest Giant in Town*, as well as a novel called *The Giants and the Joneses*. Both featured very big and very small characters. This sparked an idea for another story in which big and small animals could help each other.

Years before, Julia had written some stories that used phonic sounds to help children with reading. One of these was going to feature words with an 'ai' sound, such as 'snail', 'paint' and 'trail'. Although Julia never completed that story, she still liked the idea of a snail painting a trail and this was her starting point for *The Snail and the Whale*.

At first, Julia wanted the snail to crawl through some paint so that her 'Save the Whale' trail would be visible, but she couldn't think of how this would happen, so she decided she'd just stick with a natural, colourless trail. 'Axel can somehow make it show up,' she thought – and of course he did.

The Snail and the Whale is influenced by a poem by Edward Lear called 'The Jumblies', about a group of adventurous characters who go to sea in a sieve even though their friends try to discourage them.

Julia Says . . .

"I've always loved stories that feature characters that are both very big and very small, so the thought of a snail and a whale made me very happy."

Line illustration from 'The Jumblies' by Edward Lear.

Julia Says . . .

"This is one of my favourite stories I have written, perhaps because I feel I have captured something of the soulful whimsy of the Edward Lear poems I enjoyed as a child."

Axel was very pleased when he first read the story and found that it had an ocean setting. He had spent so much time painting trees and leaves for their previous books that the sea was something new and exciting. There were few murky, stormy skies either – just the vast ocean and the big wide world. Axel enjoyed painting all the different landscapes that the snail and the whale discover.

He had new creatures to research, too. For this story, the body of the humpback whale had to be slightly adapted so that the snail could sit neatly on its tail.

Axel Says . . .

"The whale doesn't make sense at all, whales can't bend like that, but nobody seems to mind."

Axel also thought it would be fun to sneak in a reference to the Gruffalo somewhere. In one of the scenes, he added a child drawing a gruffalo in the sand.

As with *Monkey Puzzle*, Axel made a mini-version of *The Snail and the Whale* so that he could see at a glance how the illustrations would flow over the double-page spreads.

The Gruffalo said that no gruffalo should
Ever set foot in the deep dark wood.

The Gruffalo's Child

Welcome back to the deep dark wood where the Gruffalo is telling his daughter the story of his escape from the terrifying Mouse. The Gruffalo's Child is fascinated, and one snowy night when she can't sleep, she ignores her father's warning and tiptoes out into the wood, in the hope of catching a glimpse of the Big Bad Mouse . . .

The original 2004 hardback cover of
The Gruffalo's Child.

Following the success of *The Gruffalo*, Julia had often been asked to write a sequel, but she didn't want the Gruffalo and the mouse to become like the cartoon cat and mouse Tom and Jerry, with a series of chases and escapes, so she decided to resist unless she could hit on a good enough idea for a follow-up story. Then she started to wonder what would have become of the Gruffalo several years after his encounter with the mouse. She decided that the Gruffalo could have some children and that he would warn them about the terrifying mouse in the deep dark wood.

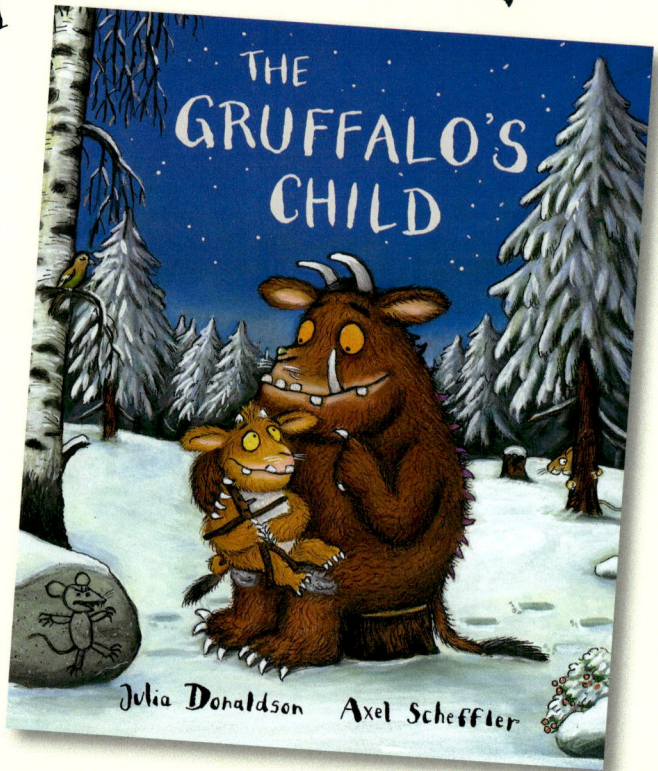

At first Julia imagined that there would be several little gruffalos in the gruffalo cave, though only one would be brave enough to go on an adventure, but the publisher persuaded her that the story would work better with just one Gruffalo's Child in the pictures.

The Gruffalo's Child would have to be brave (or foolish) enough to venture into the deep dark wood, despite her parent's warning. And she would have to meet the snake, owl and fox from the first story – and eventually the mouse, who of course, would actually be normal mouse size, not big or bad at all.

Julia Says . . .

"I liked the idea of turning the original story on its head and having the predators trick a gruffalo, but still keeping the mouse as the main trickster."

Julia then had to think of another clever trick that the mouse could play. She came up with the idea of the full moon making the mouse's shadow look scary and gigantic – like a Big Bad Mouse. But that wouldn't work on a forest floor covered in twigs and leaves. That is why Julia chose to set the story in winter, with thick white snow to make a good backdrop for the dark shadow. The snow would also be ideal for showing footprints and tracks.

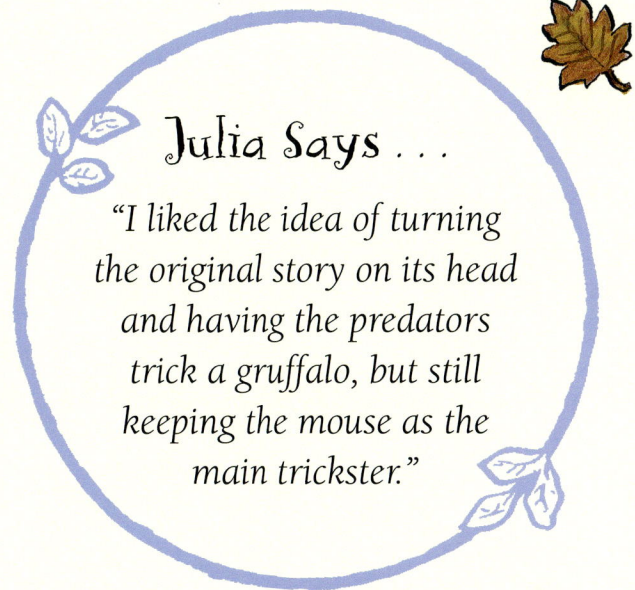

The Gruffalo's Child is scared of the Big Bad Mouse after all.

At first, Axel couldn't imagine there being a follow-up to *The Gruffalo*. But when he read Julia's story, he realised that it worked beautifully. His only slight concern was that the story was set at night in a very dark, very cold wood, which he thought might be difficult to paint. Luckily, it turned out to be easier than he'd thought. In fact, the trickiest thing was the shadow of the Big Bad Mouse in the snow – but he managed to make it look real enough to scare a gruffalo.

This early sketch shows Axel playing around with the composition of this scene to show the Big Bad Mouse's shadow.

Like Julia, Axel thought there might be a whole gruffalo family, so he drew three little gruffalos at first. The final Gruffalo's Child had a little stick doll to keep her company.

Axel tried some different groupings of his three little gruffalo children, before eventually settling on only one child.

Axel also had to think carefully about what a young gruffalo would look like. Would she already have horns? He decided that she would, but they would be smaller and rounder. He made the Child's eyes yellow instead of orange and her prickles small and pink. The poisonous wart and knobbly knees were left out as Axel decided these would probably appear later, when the Gruffalo's Child became a teenager.

In this early colour sketch, the Gruffalo's Child does not yet have her pink prickles or white chest fur.

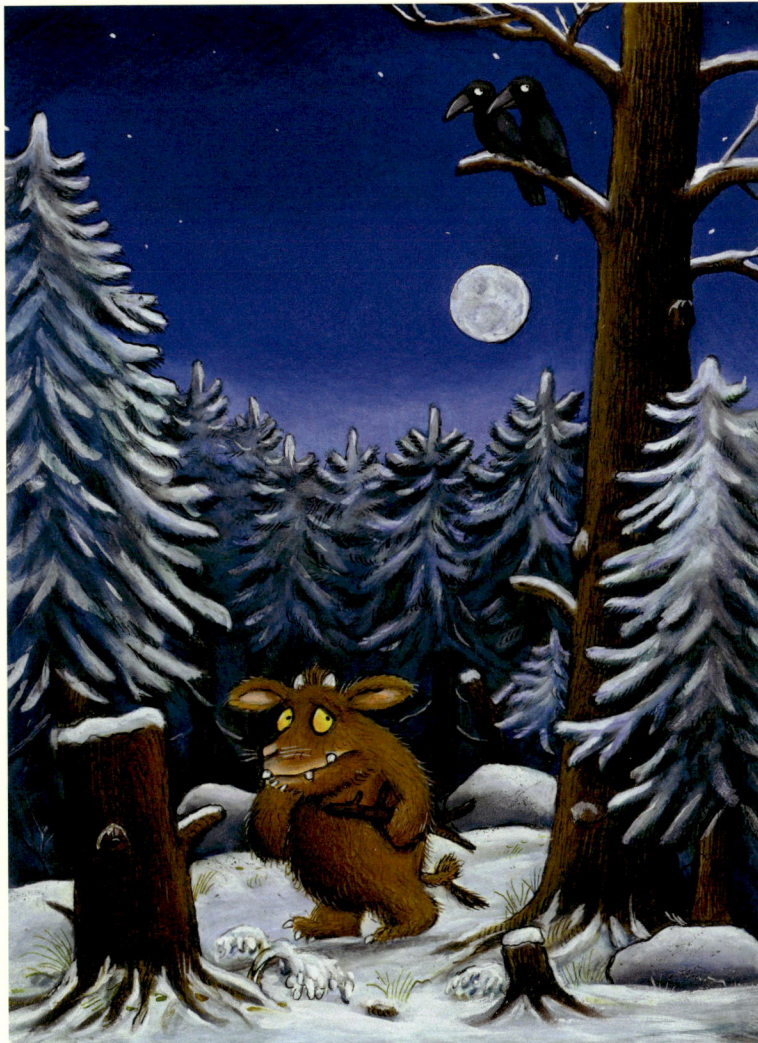

Axel's first cover design showed just the Gruffalo's Child on her own.

She looked a little lonely, so he redrew it showing her sitting on the Gruffalo's knee, which was much more comforting.

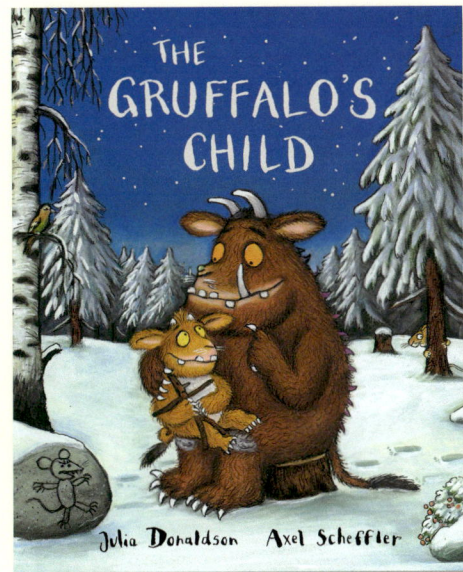

THE GRUFFALO'S CHILD

Julia Donaldson   Axel Scheffler

Once upon a time there was a boy called Charlie Cook
Who curled up in a cosy chair and read his favourite book . . .

Charlie Cook's Favourite Book

Charlie Cook is reading his favourite book about a pirate, who is reading a book about Goldilocks, who is reading a book about a knight . . . and so the story continues. From book to book, we meet aliens, thieves, queens and astronauts – and eventually a ghost, who is reading a book all about Charlie himself!

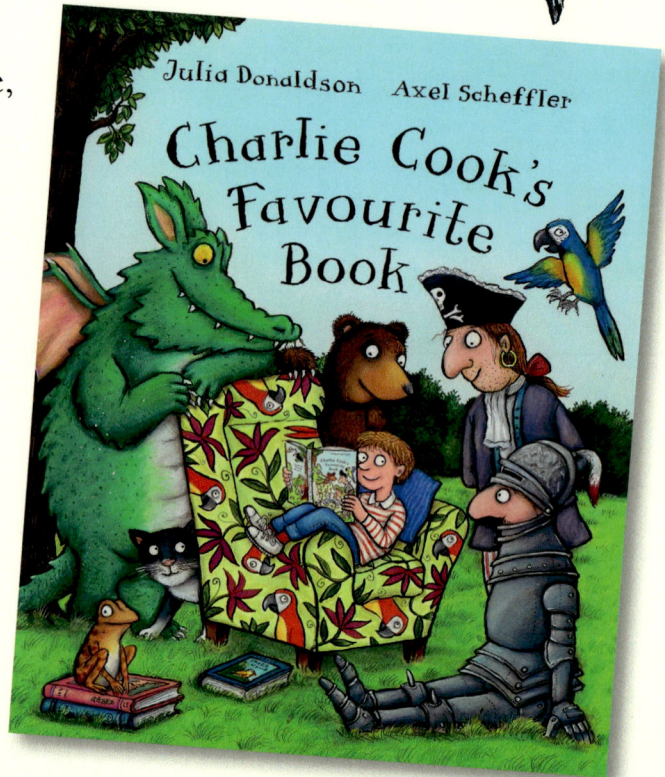

The original 2005 hardback cover of *Charlie Cook's Favourite Book*.

This book-within-a-book is quite different from all of Julia's previous stories. The clever circular tale takes us from one story to another, until we come right back to the start.

The idea came from Julia's observation that not many books include characters who are themselves reading a book. She then took this idea further, wondering 'What if someone in a book was reading a book, and that book was about someone reading a book?' and so on.

Julia loved the idea of writing a story containing worlds within worlds and was keen to feature as many different types of books as possible – including a library book because libraries are where so many of us discover our own favourite books. She wanted the story to rhyme and for each double page to end with the words 'favourite book', so she set to work finding as many rhymes as possible for the word 'book'. She came up with hook, look, shook, brook, rook, took, crook and nook – but that was not enough as she wanted the story to have twelve double pages, which is usual for a picture book. So she then hit on the idea of a favourite magazine and an encyclopedia. Magazine was an easy word to rhyme, but what could rhyme with encyclopedia? Julia was quite pleased with herself when she came up with 'greedier'.

Julia later wrote a special song called 'A World Inside a Book' based on the same idea, which can be found in another book, *A Treasury of Songs*.

This shelf of books is featured on the endpapers of *Charlie Cook's Favourite Book* and shows all the different books that appear in the story.

Axel had a lot of fun illustrating Charlie Cook's living room. If you look carefully, you can see that all the characters from the story are present in this opening scene as toys and other objects.

Later, at the end of the story, they have come to life from the pages of Charlie's book!

As with all his books, Axel made various alterations as the artwork progressed. He experimented with different looks for the Queen in the encyclopedia entry.

This early sketch shows the Queen sitting with her back to the reader whilst a team of footmen carry the cake in the background.

In the final artwork, the Queen is seated facing the reader, with her dog by her side.

For the Goldilocks and the Three Bears story, Axel painted two full colour illustrations of the bedroom that were slightly different before combining elements of both to create the final artwork.

Axel also painted different versions of the pirate chief and his parrot, which was originally red. Even Charlie Cook himself looked a little different in the early versions Axel drew and painted; Charlie's original grey and brown clothes were brightened up and became a striped top and trainers.

This version of Charlie Cook shows him reading a book about a pirate who is also reading a book . . .

"Sorry I'm late. I was riding on a seahorse.
Sorry I'm late. I was flying with a ray.
Sorry I'm late. I was diving with a dolphin."
Tiddler told a different story every day.

Tiddler

Tiddler is a little fish who tells the tallest tales in the ocean. But did he really ride a seahorse and meet a mermaid? None of the other fish believe him. One day, Tiddler gets caught in a net and, when the fishermen throw him back into the ocean, finds himself completely lost. Luckily, he overhears some other sea creatures retelling his own stories. Can he follow the story trail through the ocean all the way back home?

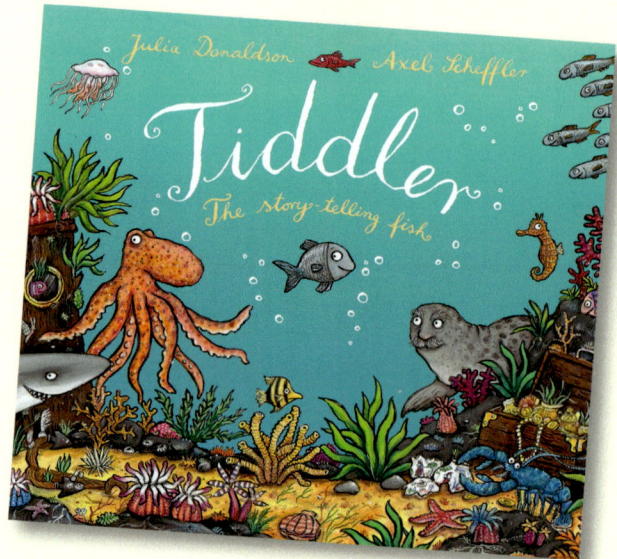

The original 2007 hardback cover of *Tiddler*.

Unlike many of Julia's stories, which can take a very long time for her to think about and develop, the idea that a trail of stories could lead a lost fish home came to her very quickly. This idea appealed to her because, like Tiddler, she is a storyteller whose tales spread far and wide.

Tiddler's best friend is Little Johnny Dory and, at the end of the book, Johnny tells Tiddler's story to 'a writer friend'. This was of course to be Julia herself, and Julia had imagined that she would be pictured in a boat with the fish popping out of the sea to tell her the story. But Axel decided instead that the scene should be set underwater – Johnny Dory's natural habitat – so he drew Julia in diving gear, with a helmet and flippers!

Julia Says . . .

"Making up stories is Tiddler's salvation – it's the storyline of all my books that I feel is one of my most original."

This scene from the final book shows Julia dressed in scuba-diving gear with a notepad and pencil.

Researching the ocean and choosing which of its many sea creatures to write about was great fun for Julia. She knew that Axel would enjoy illustrating the underwater scenes full of colourful ocean creatures, from crabs and turtles to seals and squid.

Axel thought it would be fun to include a Gruffalo fish in the artwork as a reference to their most famous character.

Julia Says . . .

"All the fish in the story are real ones – except for the Gruffalo fish, which Axel sneaked in."

Axel had illustrated sea scenes before, but a story set completely underwater was a first for him. He wondered if all his creatures should be tinted blue to show that they were surrounded by water, but later decided against it.

Using Julia's research for reference, Axel quickly drew pages covered in fish, each with slightly different fins, tails and facial expressions.

Axel wondered whether there might be a problem with the fish being from different parts of the ocean, but the editor suggested that Tiddler's school was rather a good one and therefore fish came from all over the ocean to attend!

Drawing a skate taking a register was tricky to depict, but Axel managed it perfectly.

Tiddler himself presented quite a challenge for the book's cover: being small and grey, he could easily disappear, but with a clever layout and some bubbles, Tiddler became the star of the show and stood out from all the colourful creatures around him.

Axel did lots of different sketches for the cover, but he eventually ran out of ideas!

... Well, I'm running out of ideas to be honest ...

Luckily, he eventually found a winning design, with Tiddler in the centre of the cover, surrounded by his friends.

"I'm Stick Man, I'm Stick Man,
I'M STICK MAN! That's me.
And I want to go home to the family tree."

Stick Man

Stick Man lives in his family tree, with his Stick Lady Love and three stick children. But the world is a dangerous place for a stick man. One day, he is out for a jog when a lively dog picks him up. Then a girl throws him into a river; a swan weaves him into her nest; a man uses him as a flagpole for a sandcastle. Poor Stick Man is passed from one character to another for all kinds of different uses – he even ends up in the grate of a fire. Will he ever get back home to the family tree?

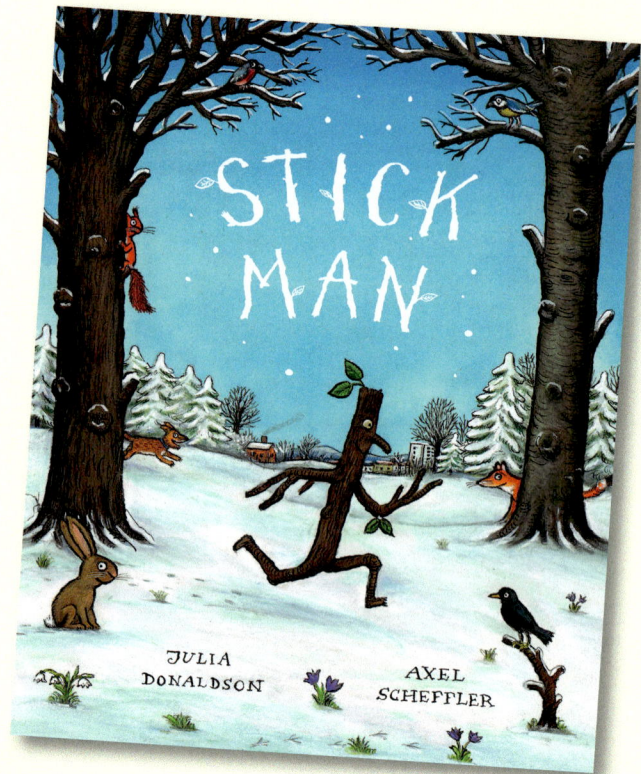

The original 2008 hardback cover of *Stick Man*.

The idea for *Stick Man* first came to Julia when she saw Axel's illustrations for *The Gruffalo's Child*. He had given the Gruffalo's Child a little doll to carry around, made from a stick from the deep dark wood.

Julia cast her mind back to when her sons were little, and they would pick up a stick and pretend that it was a sword or a violin or some other imaginary object. A stick could be anything at all, even a person.

Julia conjured up a whole Stick family who lived together in a tree – a family tree, of course! She did consider basing the story on various fairy tales, in which case one of the Three Little Pigs would have used Stick Man to build his house of wood. But as her idea progressed, it became a tale rooted in everyday life with humans and animals controlling Stick Man's fate.

Julia Says . . .

"Our children used to love picking up sticks and playing with them. That was where my idea started – I wanted the stick to become all sorts of different things for different characters."

To add a sense of danger, Julia had him being taken far away from his family, but she wasn't sure at first how he would find his way home. She liked the idea of him being dropped back into his family tree. Then it came to her: why not have Santa Claus bring him back in time for Christmas? This worked well with the timeline of the story, which celebrates the seasons, with scenes set in spring, summer, autumn and winter.

Stick Man being rescued from the fireplace by Santa Claus.

Axel was delighted that Julia had written a story based on the little stick toy in *The Gruffalo's Child*. Working out all the Stick family characters was another thing entirely, though. The bodies were fairly simple to draw, but giving them all different characters and expressions to make them look different from one another was not so easy.

For the main character, Axel sketched a few possible stick men with different types of hand. Some resembled twigs and others were shaped like human hands. Stick Man ended up with 'twiggy' limbs and two leaves on his head for 'hair'. Should the leaves change colour throughout the seasons, or would Stick Man be evergreen? After much discussion, it was decided that in autumn, Stick Man's leaves would turn from green to brown.

Axel Says . . .

"I really like the way this story moves through the different seasons and settings."

A series of Axel's Stick Man character sketches.

Axel decided to draw leaves for the Stick family's bedding rather than blankets, as it felt more natural.

A scene from the story showing
Axel's unique Santa.

The Christmas scenes posed a problem as
Christmas is celebrated differently all over
the world. For example, the stockings
featured on some spreads are not used
everywhere. Even Santa does not look
exactly the same everywhere in the world,
so Axel found his own version of Santa,
with a red suit and green gloves.

Although most international editions
used the same cover as the UK original,
the US edition wanted to make the image
even more festive and so added baubles
to the front cover and Santa hats to the
characters on the back.

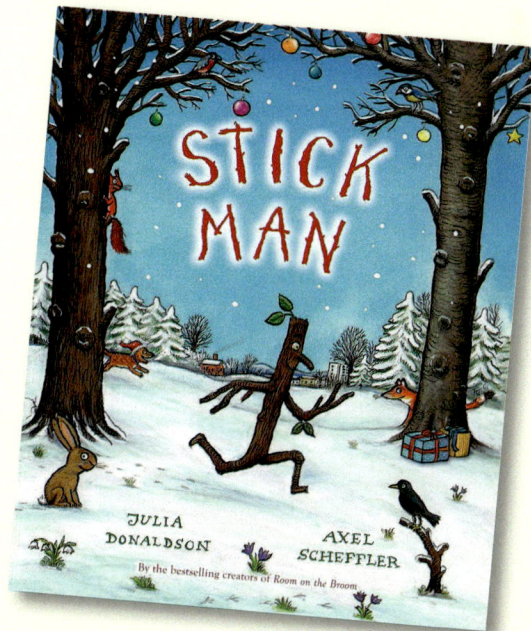

The US edition, published by
Arthur A. Levine Books, 2009.

99

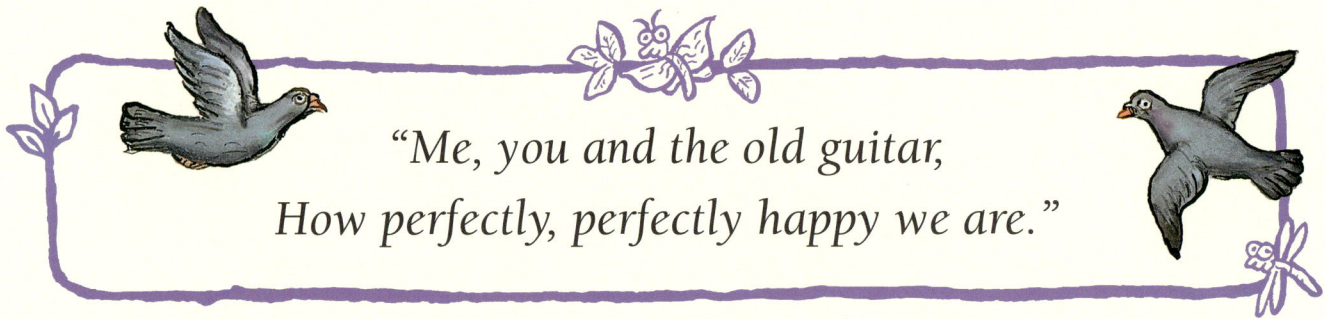

"Me, you and the old guitar,
How perfectly, perfectly happy we are."

Tabby McTat

Tabby McTat is purr-fectly happy, singing along with Fred the busker all day long. But one day Fred and McTat are separated. McTat eventually finds a new home with a lady cat called Sock and they have three lovely kittens together. As the kittens grow up, McTat teaches them his old busking song. One day, McTat finds Fred by the river and they sing together once again. But McTat misses Sock and his new home. What can he do?

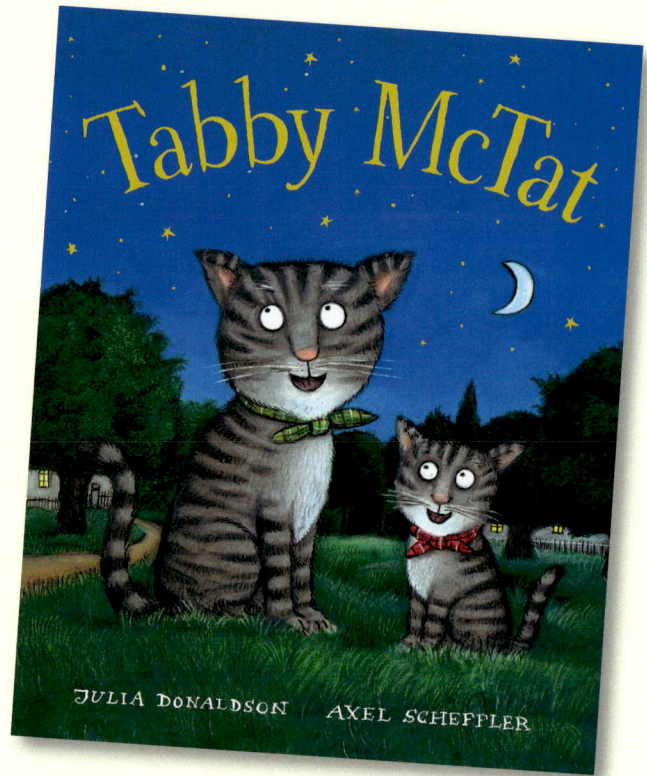

The original 2009 hardback cover of *Tabby McTat*.

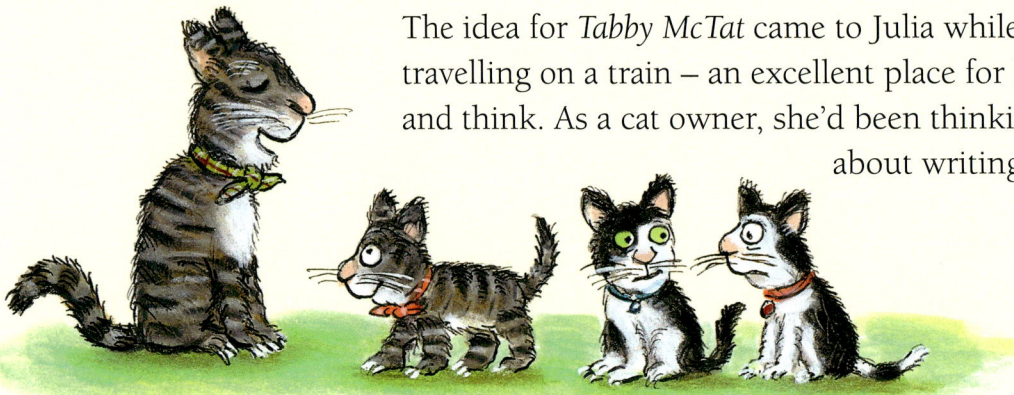

The idea for *Tabby McTat* came to Julia while she was travelling on a train – an excellent place for her to sit and think. As a cat owner, she'd been thinking for a while about writing a cat story.

100

Julia wanted the cat in the story to have an owner, and for the two of them to become separated for some reason. But who would the owner be – a cook, a train driver, even a burglar? Then, thinking back to her street-singing days, Julia decided to make Fred a busker. This meant she could write a special song for McTat and Fred to sing. Julia's husband, Malcolm, suggested that this song could be passed down to the next generation. So at the end of the book one of Tabby McTat's sons, a kitten called Samuel Sprat, becomes the new busking cat.

Julia Says . . .

"I am a cat-lover, and I also used to go busking with my husband, Malcolm. So I put a cat and a busker together in this story. When I wrote it, we had three cats – Campsie, and her two sons, Gizmo and Goblin."

Julia now has two cats called Tabitha and McTat – just like the busking cat in the story.

Tabby McTat being reunited with his old friend, Fred the busker.

Unlike Julia, Axel didn't own a cat when he was illustrating the story, but he knew enough about pet cats to create the friendly feline we now know as Tabby McTat. If you look carefully, you'll see that McTat has no teeth at all. Axel originally gave him a lovely set of teeth, but they looked a little bit too sharp and spiky – so now McTat is toothless!

As with all his books, Axel sketched different versions of the characters.

Could be ved with white doh but I think should be Tarbon

In this version, the cats have little pointed teeth.

Axel then had to decide what the setting would be. The editor suggested a village, but Axel thought an urban setting would be a more realistic backdrop for a busker. His city is loosely based on London, but it could be anywhere in the world with its skyscrapers, winding river and litter-strewn streets.

Axel Says . . .

"I find it quite hard to illustrate stories set in the real world because it never looks quite like the real world anyway!"

The final scene of the story also changed quite a bit during the development stages. In this early version, Fred and Samuel are busking for a happy audience, but Axel felt that something was missing from the scene – Tabby McTat and Sock, of course!

McTat & Socks to be added

The image was reworked to allow more space for the text and to give more of a focus to the central characters. A purr-fect ending!

Zog, the biggest dragon, was the keenest one by far.
He tried his hardest every day to win a golden star.

Zog

Zog is the keenest young dragon to attend Madam Dragon's school, trying his hardest at everything in the hope of winning a golden star. But he's also the most accident-prone, flying into trees and even setting his own wing on fire. Luckily, a mysterious little girl always comes by and patches up his bumps and bruises. Will she be able to help him with his toughest test yet – capturing a princess?

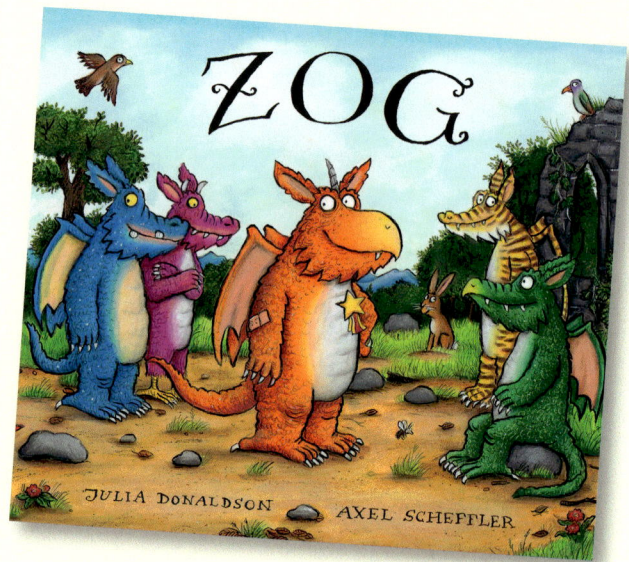

The original 2010 hardback cover of *Zog*.

Although there is a dragon in *Room on the Broom*, Julia had never before created a dragon hero. Her editor had begged her to write a dragon story, so she made a list of 'dragon ideas' and hit on the name Madam Dragon, whose sound appealed to her. But who could Madam Dragon be? Julia had various thoughts, including a shopkeeper, but eventually decided to make her a teacher.

Axel drew this picture of Julia writing the story with little dragons playing at her feet.

The plot came to Julia little by little. Zog would be a dragon at the school, learning different skills, including flying and fire-breathing. She thought that, in the fairy-tale tradition, it would be nice to include a princess and a knight in the story, and that Zog would keep meeting one or other of them and become friends. Perhaps they could eat marshmallows together, toasted by Zog's fiery breath? But when Julia's husband, Malcolm – who happens to be a doctor – said that sounded a bit tame, Julia wondered what might happen if her princess had ambitions to be a doctor too. It all came together, and the Flying Doctors were born.

Zog and his school friends learning how to fly.

Axel has always enjoyed making up imaginary creatures, so Zog gave him the perfect opportunity to create a whole class of fantastical dragons. As usual, he sketched many different dragons beforehand, not only for Zog, but for all the other pupils at Madam Dragon's school. Each was a different colour and a slightly different shape.

Axel Says . . .

"I tried out several types of dragon. I had a bit of freedom there, as most people haven't ever seen one. I gave Zog a kind of beaky snout in the end, just like some dinosaurs have."

Axel had lots of fun painting different types of dragon in preparation for this book.

106

Zog is now a vibrant orange colour, but in Julia's first draft he was called Zog the zig-zag dragon. The zig-zags would have been an interesting challenge for Axel to illustrate. However, the problem of translating 'zig-zag' into different languages meant that it was dropped – and we ended up with simply Zog.

When Julia and the editor were discussing what to replace 'zig-zag' with, they decided on 'biggest' rather than 'smallest' because they wanted to challenge the idea that a picture-book hero is often cute and little.

Zog needs a little more practice flying!

One thing that Axel spent a lot of time on in this story was working out how to draw the characters at different ages. A lot of time passes by during Zog's school years – time in which both the little girl and the dragons grow into young adults. They still had to look recognisable, however.

Zog and his friends are grown up – and he finally receives his gold star!

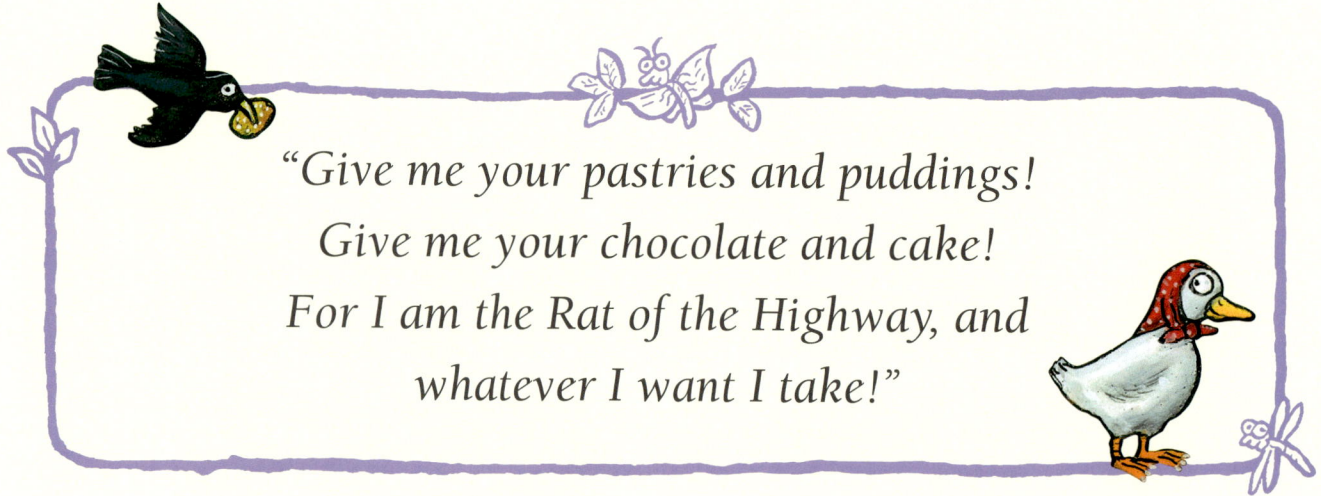

"Give me your pastries and puddings!
Give me your chocolate and cake!
For I am the Rat of the Highway, and
whatever I want I take!"

The Highway Rat

The Highway Rat rides along the roads, stealing food from the animal travellers. He even steals his own horse's hay. The animals all grow thinner and thinner, but no one dares stand up to him. That is, until a clever duck manages to outwit him with a trick based on an echo. She lures him into a hilltop cave, then escapes on his horse and returns to her hungry friends, feeding them with the Rat's stolen snacks.

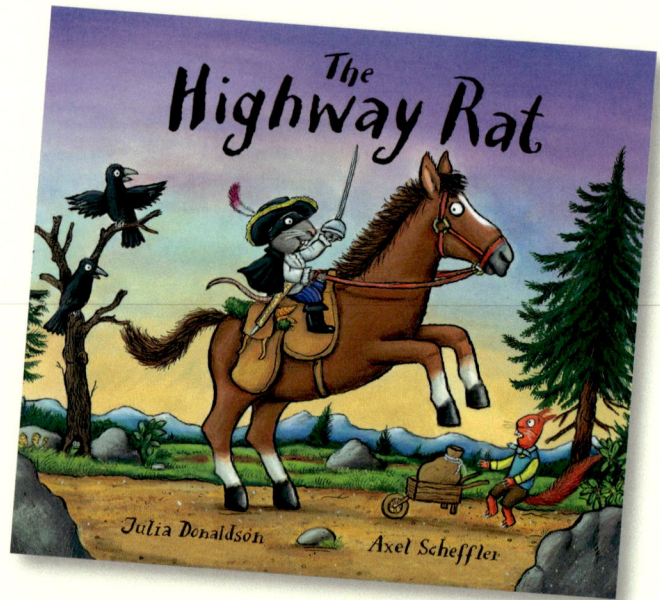

The original 2011 hardback cover of *The Highway Rat*.

Julia wanted to write about a villain as there hadn't been one in her most recent books (apart from a thief who only had a small role in *Tabby McTat*). A highway robber came to mind, but what sort of animal would he be? She considered a wolf or a fox, but thought either of them would look odd on a horse, whereas a rat could sit neatly on the saddle.

108

There is a famous poem called, 'The Highwayman',
written in 1906 by Alfred Noyes. Julia studied this
poem at school and loved the rhythm of the lines,
which sounded just like the highwayman galloping
along on his horse:

And the highwayman came riding –
Riding– riding–
The highwayman came riding, up to the old inn door.

The Highway Rat goes riding, riding, riding, too, and
Julia has cleverly used the same rhythmic pattern in
her verse as a tribute to the original poem.

Julia Says . . .

"Although the Rat
is such a rotter, I can't
help having a soft
spot for him."

109

Out of all of Julia's stories, *The Highway Rat* was one of Axel's absolute favourites to illustrate. Over the years, he has realised that he just loves drawing rodents – you'll find a red squirrel in almost all of his books. Drawing and painting the evil Rat with his mask and sword was highly enjoyable. The Rat's horse was a little more difficult, but Axel pulled it off, of course!

An early sketch of the Highway Rat on his horse.

Although Axel wanted to keep many of the scenes very simple and bold, the feasting spread is a triumph of invention and fun, with lots of details to spot, including some dancing ants. It is packed full of Axel's signature wit and warmth.

110

Despite the Highway Rat being a baddie, we also need to sympathise with him and find him funny. Axel handled this expertly by putting some of the more sinister elements into the surrounding landscape instead of into the character himself. The brooding skies, broken trees and lurking crows all work to create the atmosphere.

Axel did this early colour sketch which isn't a scene from the final book, but he used it to play around with creating the right atmosphere for the landscape.

A little while after the book was first published, it was pointed out that the Highway Rat on the cover had not one sword but two – something which had gone completely unnoticed by Axel and the editor. This was corrected, and the Rat now wields a single blade when galloping down the highway.

On the original cover we see the tip of one sword peeping out of the end of the scabbard, and another being wielded by the Highway Rat.

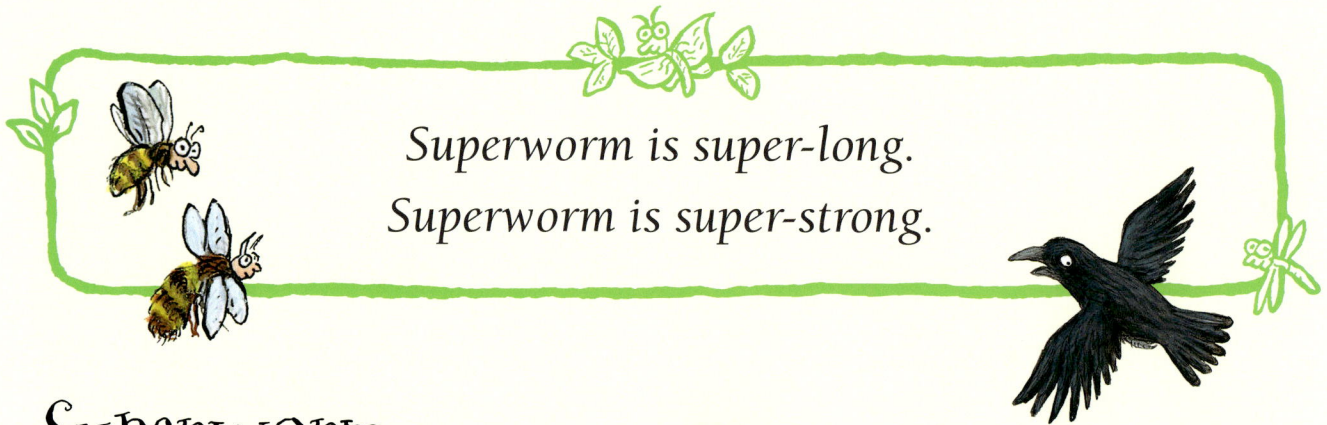

Superworm is super-long.
Superworm is super-strong.

Superworm

All the garden creatures love brave, kind Superworm. He helps everyone, from Baby Toad to the tiniest beetle. Then one day, the evil Wizard Lizard kidnaps Superworm and forces him to look for buried treasure. Will Superworm ever be able to escape? Perhaps it's time for his garden friends to repay his help . . .

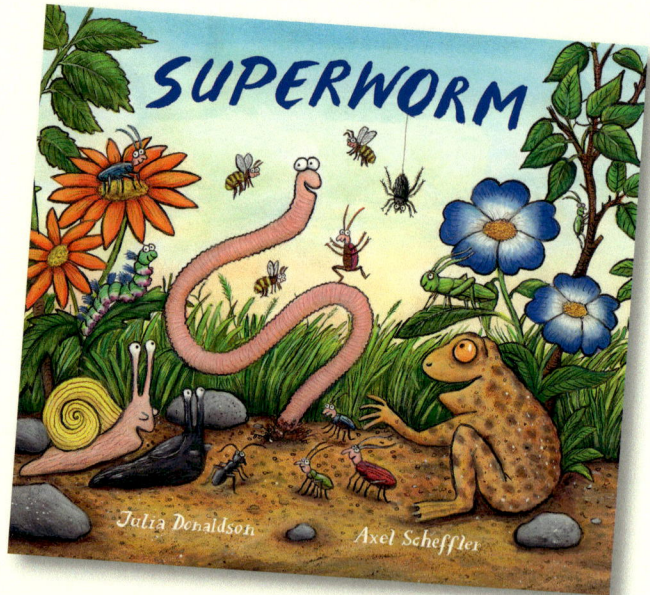

The original 2012 hardback cover of *Superworm*.

Julia has always loved the way Axel puts extra details into his illustrations, including lots of expressive little bugs and butterflies hovering in the background.

Superworm with some beetle friends.

These creatures inspired Julia to write a story about garden insects and minibeasts, as she knew Axel would illustrate them perfectly.

She had also never written a story led by a superhero character and decided it was about time. She combined this with the garden setting and came up with the character of Superworm. Julia also had fun creating another baddie in the shape of Wizard Lizard, who is much more evil than the Highway Rat, whom she couldn't help liking just a little bit.

Julia Says . . .

"Axel is brilliant at drawing bugs and had sneaked a lot of them into our previous picture books, so I decided to write a story all about them."

Everyone working together to carry off the evil Wizard Lizard.

Having a worm superhero as the star of the story presented Axel with quite a challenge. Worms don't have features that an illustrator can use to create character and expression. How could he make Superworm look like a brave superhero?

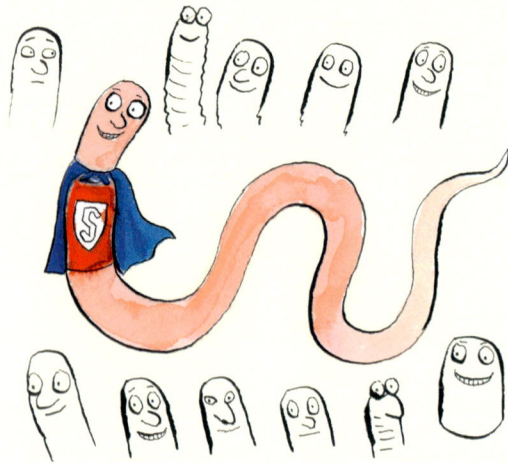

Axel Says . . .

"Worms have no arms, legs, noses, ears or anything much, so all the expression had to be in his eyes and mouth."

Axel tried drawing Superworm with a cape, but decided that it didn't look quite right. Superworm ended up cape-less, but after a lot of tries, Axel did manage to get lots of expression into his eyes and mouth. At least Superworm's body was quite simple for Axel to transform into a skipping rope, a lasso and a fishing line!

When Axel saw that Julia had written an Earwig Aunt into the story, unusually he asked Julia if she might change the insect to something else. He hates earwigs! Julia had a think, but no other two-syllable insect name sounded quite right before 'Aunt' (which conveniently rhymes with 'chant'). So Earwig Aunt stayed, but you will never find an earwig in any of Axel's other illustrations.

For this story, Axel used a bold style, with characters often placed on a white background, zooming in to make the creatures large in their world. We're used to seeing Axel's big landscapes, but this miniature world allowed him to go close up, making all the characters endearing, even though they're mostly creepy-crawlies.

Harry loved Betty, and Betty loved Harry,
So Harry said, "Betty, my beauty, let's marry!"

The Scarecrows' Wedding

Two scarecrows, Betty O'Barley and Harry O'Hay, are planning the perfect wedding. When Harry goes off in search of some pink flowers, wicked scarecrow Reginald Rake has plans to ruin their special day. Can Harry race to the rescue so that he and Betty can enjoy the wedding of their dreams?

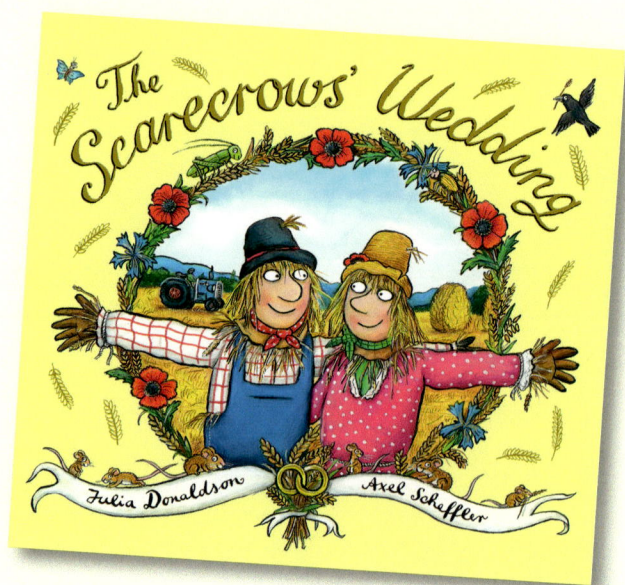

The original 2014 hardback cover of *The Scarecrows' Wedding*.

Julia Says . . .

"I was really keen to have a strong central female character, so I created Betty O'Barley, the scarecrow."

Julia really wanted to have a lead female character in this book, so Betty came into her mind before Harry. Weddings had recently featured in Julia's life, as her sons Alastair and Jerry were now both married, which is perhaps why she decided to write her first love story. While the story is very romantic, it also turned into a nail-biting adventure!

The details of the story took a while to get right. Julia wanted Harry to disappear for a while so that the farmer replaces him with wicked villain, Reginald. But what could Harry be doing all that time? Would he be locked up in a garden shed? Or arrested for taking something from a washing line?

Eventually, she hit upon the task of Harry finding flowers and water for the wedding. Harry's bucket of pondwater would be perfect to put out the fire that Reginald causes. The story came together in the end, and now Julia and her husband, Malcolm, have fun dressing up as Harry and Betty in their regular shows.

Julia and Malcolm happily in love as scarecrows Harry and Betty, on stage at Edinburgh International Festival.

The colours in this book are bright and summery – a contrast to lots of Julia and Axel's other stories full of stormy skies.

Drawing scarecrows for the first time presented Axel with a bit of a conundrum. How would the scarecrows move about? In real life, they are usually tied to sticks. Julia imagined that Betty and Harry would hop about on their poles, but Axel wasn't sure. In the end, Axel gave them little peg legs to move about on, which look entirely right for a scarecrow.

Axel Says . . .

"I ignored the logic, as I do in all the books – it's a world where anything can happen!"

In these early development sketches, Axel drew the scarecrows on poles like real scarecrows.

The problem of the scarecrows' hands was solved by putting gloves on the ends of their sleeves. But what about their faces? Axel decided to give them heads made out of sacks so that he could draw human-like features on them.

BETTY   HARRY   REGINALD

Axel also tried some different versions of Harry's and Betty's outfits, before doing the final illustrations. Harry's necktie and patch on his trousers changed from green to red, but Betty ended up with a complete outfit change! The dark green dress she is wearing here became a spotty pink dress with lace ruffles in the final book – and now it's hard to imagine her looking any different.

An early colour version of this scene from the beginning of the story.

For the original cover design of the hardback – which came out in the summer – Harry and Betty are surrounded by a garland of fresh flowers and corn, giving the book a fresh, summery look.

An early sketch of the cover design for the hardback edition of the book.

When the paperback edition of the book was published a year later, the publisher asked Axel to come up with a different cover design. This more scenic approach includes lots of animals and even a tractor to show off the farmyard setting.

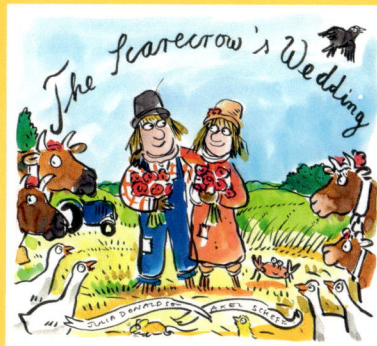

A colour sketch of the paperback cover.

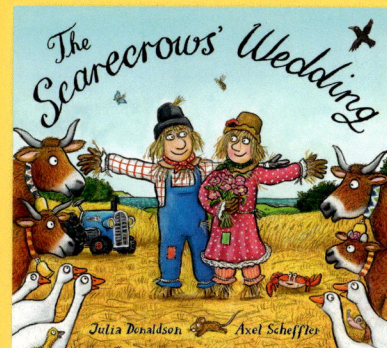

The final paperback cover, published in 2015.

Meet the Flying Doctors – a dragon, knight and girl.
Their names are Gadabout the Great, and Zog, and Princess Pearl.

Zog and the Flying Doctors

In this sequel to *Zog*, the Flying Doctors are very happy helping all sorts of creatures, from a sunburnt mermaid to a unicorn with two horns, and even a lion with the flu. But Pearl's uncle, the King, disapproves of princesses being doctors and imprisons her in his palace. Zog and Gadabout visit her every night, and when the King falls ill it's up to the Flying Doctors to find the ingredients for the cure and change the King's mind for good.

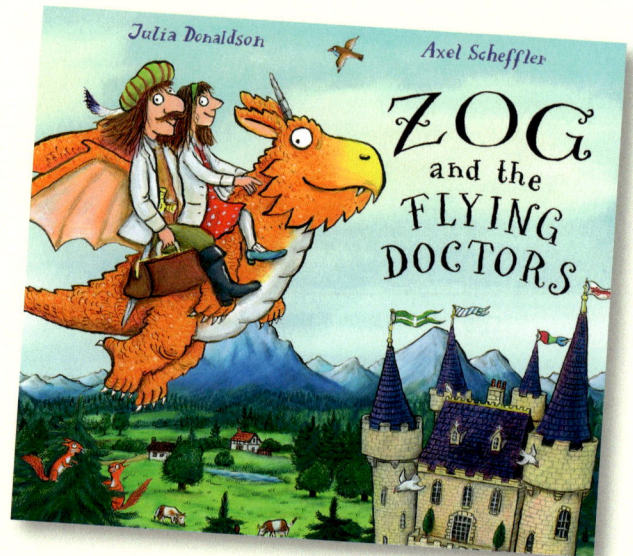

The original 2016 hardback cover of *Zog and the Flying Doctors.*

Julia doesn't often write sequels to her picture-book stories, but the ending of Zog got her thinking. As Zog, Pearl and Gadabout went zig-zagging off together, she couldn't help wondering what the future held for them.

Zog is good at flying, but still hasn't quite got the hang of landing!

In this second story, all is resolved. We meet wonderful new characters and Pearl gets a chance to show what a great doctor she has become when she cures the king's orange fever. As always, Julia is brilliant at reworking traditional fairy-tale characters with a modern twist and Pearl's career change from princess to doctor is a great example of this.

Julia Says . . .

"Zog is an adventure story, so it lent itself to a sequel, unlike some of my other stories, which are more like fables. The ending of Zog is a new beginning."

Julia's editor was at first a little worried that readers might feel squeamish about Sir Gadabout using his sword as a surgical instrument to saw off the unicorn's unwanted horn, so Julia changed 'He sawed the extra horn off' to 'He cut the horn off gently', which sounded a bit less alarming.

The Flying Doctors helping their unicorn patient.

Axel loves drawing imaginary creatures and is always delighted when one of Julia's stories gives him the chance to delve into the fantasy genre. Even though he never gets involved in Julia's writing process, he did mention that he'd like to draw some mythical beasts. He was thinking of sphinxes and phoenixes, but Julia came up with a mermaid and a unicorn.

For *Zog and the Flying Doctors*, Axel added white coats to Princess Pearl and Sir Gadabout's outfits to show that they were now proper doctors. He then had the tricky task of creating characters who were rather poorly, including a two-horned unicorn, a sunburnt mermaid and a sneezing lion.

Axel's illustration of Princess Pearl treating the mermaid's sunburn.

Julia's text originally mentioned a 'mountain lion's sneeze', so that's what Axel drew in his first rough sketch.

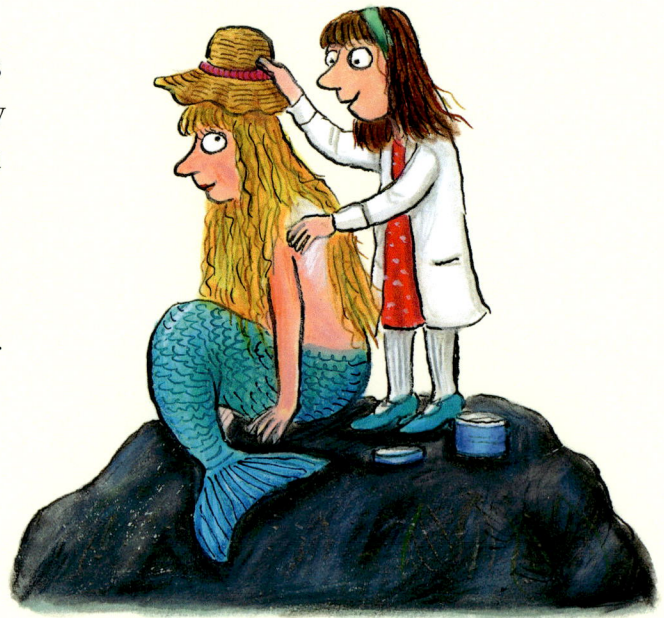

Axel's first sketch showing a poorly mountain lion.

However, in the end it was felt that a more familiar lion, complete with mane, was appropriate for the story. The text then was changed to 'a mighty lion's sneeze'.

122

In Axel's first sketches for the story, he thought Pearl and Gadabout should treat human patients as well as animals.

But he later changed his mind and decided all the patients should be animals. Here, Pearl is giving medicine to a wolf and Gadabout is bandaging the leg of an injured deer.

Axel Says . . .

"I didn't expect that Julia would write a sequel to Zog, but I really enjoyed returning to this fairy-tale world."

> *"We're the ugly five, we're the ugly five.*
> *Everyone flees when they see us arrive."*

The Ugly Five

The animals are relaxing on the sunny African plain, making a beautiful scene. That is, until a wildebeest comes along, with her gingery beard and spindly legs. Over the next pages, she is joined by four other ugly animals – a spotted hyena, a lappet-faced vulture, a warthog and a marabou stork. But not everyone thinks they are ugly: their babies love their parents because they are kind, cuddly, brave and strong – perfect just the way they are!

Some years ago, Julia was lucky enough to visit South Africa on a book tour. Afterwards, she and her husband Malcolm went on a safari, hoping to see some of the Big Five: the lion, leopard, rhinoceros, elephant and African buffalo.

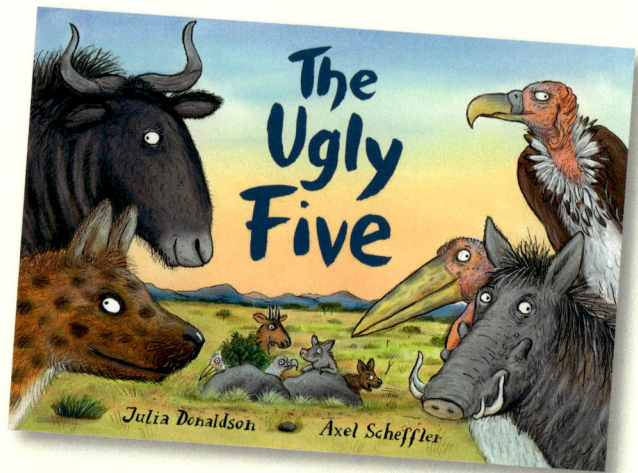

The original 2018 hardback cover of *The Ugly Five*.

lion

elephant

African buffalo

rhinoceros

leopard

Julia Says . . .

"We saw some wildebeest and the guide told us they are one of the Ugly Five. I pricked up my ears immediately and the guide told us what the other animals are."

Julia hadn't been expecting to get an idea for a new book, but that's exactly what happened when she and Malcolm spotted some wildebeest and their guide told them about the other Ugly Five animals. Immediately, Julia knew what story she would write, and she started work almost as soon as they got home.

The Ugly Five are the wildebeest, spotted hyena, warthog, lappet-faced vulture and the marabou stork.

Axel researched all of the Ugly Five thoroughly before he started sketching. His challenge was to work out how to show characters who have some distinctly unappealing habits: the marabou stork has legs covered in poo; the hyena crunches on bones; and the vulture likes food that's been dead for a while.

Somehow Axel managed to make all these odd-looking animals look strangely endearing. He even squeezed some of his trademark squirrels into the book.

Axel Says . . .

"It was suggested at some point that the ugliness of the creatures should be even more extreme and exaggerated, but I felt they should look more naturalistic."

If you look hard, you will see three small South African ground squirrels scampering along in the foreground!

Axel experimented with his style to work out how realistic the animals should be. As you can see here, he tried a more caricatured style before settling on a more naturalistic version of the animals.

Then the question was how fierce should the animals look? Although they're meant to be ugly, Axel didn't want to make them too terrifying for young readers.

The hyena looks a little too fierce in this colour sketch.

Julia specified that the lappet-faced vulture lived in a powder puff tree, but Axel was unsure where he might find one to sketch. Luckily, there were plenty of reference photos online for him to make sure he got it right.

The vulture at home in the powder puff tree.

127

"Never, never play with the Smoos.
They sleep in holes. They wear strange shoes."

The Smeds and the Smoos

On a faraway planet, two young aliens meet and soon fall in love. But Janet is a red Smed and Bill is a blue Smoo – and Smeds and Smoos are sworn enemies. Their families forbid them to see one another, so Janet and Bill decide to run away. When they finally return home, they have a surprise in store – a new baby, who is neither red nor blue, but purple!

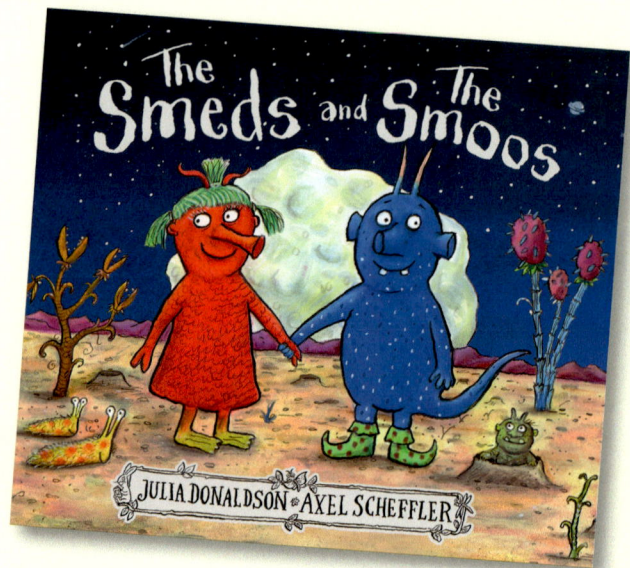

The original 2019 hardback cover of *The Smeds and the Smoos*.

Axel Says . . .

"Julia has written about every subject on earth, from sticks and snails to highway robbers, so we had to move into outer space!"

For many years, Julia had been mulling over an idea for a story about two rival alien families. She'd always really liked the amusing little aliens Axel had drawn in *Charlie Cook's Favourite Book*, and thought they'd work brilliantly in a longer story. Gradually, the idea came together, and Julia finally sat down and wrote her outer-space adventure.

Shakespeare's famous play, *Romeo and Juliet*, was at the back of Julia's mind, too, with its tale of young lovers from two families at war with each other. However, unlike the tragic Shakespeare play, Julia has given *The Smeds and the Smoos* a happy ending, in which both families come together and end up the best of friends.

Originally, Julia was going to call the rival tribes the Reds and Blues, but she changed that to the rhyming Smeds and Smoos, and went on to invent lots of other nonsense words, in the style of her favourite nonsense poet, Edward Lear.

Julia Says . . .

"Because this story is set in imaginary space, I could have fun making up the names of all the different planets, like Lurglestrop and Klaboo."

Having aliens as his theme meant that Axel could be incredibly free and creative in his ideas – apart from making sure that the Smeds and the Smoos were in reds and blues, of course. He drew lots of aliens to try out different ideas. At first, he thought that the Smeds might have an aquatic appearance because they live in a lake.

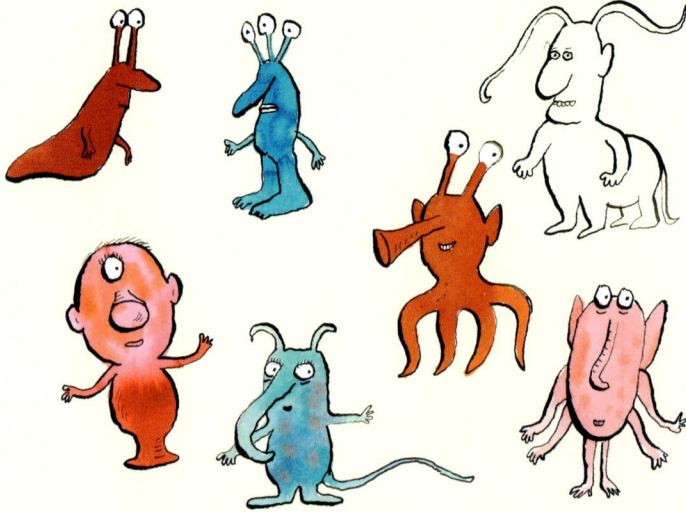

Axel Says . . .

"I enjoyed having the freedom to draw those crazy aliens, as much as Julia enjoyed making up all those nonsense words."

130

An early version of Janet shows her with scales, webbed feet and a tail fin. However, she finally evolved into a dress-shaped alien with fetching green hair.

An early illustration of Bill and a very fishy-looking Janet.

In this version, Axel played around with different facial features. Bill has a long crocodile-like snout and Janet has tall antennae and a droopy nose.

Grandmother Smoo drinking tea with Bill.

Another challenge was Grandmother Smoo. In the story, it says that Smoos don't have hair, which meant it was surprisingly hard to make her look elderly. In the end, Axel gave her head a bun-like shape, along with spectacles and a stick. Grandfather Smed was adorned with a wiry beard along with his spectacles.

Grandfather Smed saying goodnight to Janet.

Axel really values the overall message of the book, that we should learn to live together and appreciate our similarities and differences. He was illustrating the story shortly after Britain voted to withdraw from the European Union and therefore he and Julia dedicated the book 'To all the children of Europe'.

*There once lived a troll and a ghost and a witch.
They were horrible baddies all three.*

The Baddies

The Baddies are a ghost, a witch and a troll who adore being bad and are always fighting over who is the worst. When a little girl moves into a nearby cottage, the Baddies can't wait to terrify her. A mouse suggests a competition to see who can steal the girl's blue spotted hanky. But this little girl isn't so easily scared as they'd hoped . . .

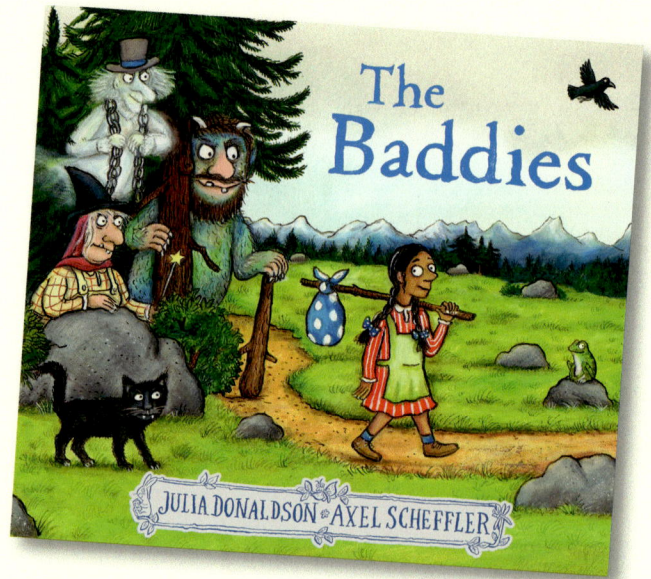

The original 2022 hardback cover of *The Baddies*.

Julia's previous two books with Axel hadn't included a villain, so she felt it was time to introduce one. But why stick at just one? Once she had hit on the idea of three rival baddies, she needed to decide who they would be. Various possibilities came to mind, including a wolf, a goblin and a giant.

In the end, she decided on three characters who would have quite different ways of being bad: a bullying troll, a scary ghost, and a witch who could use magic to turn people to stone.

The story has some similarities to Aesop's fable, 'The Wind and the Sun', in which the wind and the sun try to outdo each other by seeing who can make a man remove his cloak first. As Julia has often said, traditional stories can be wonderful sources of inspiration for writers.

Julia Says . . .

"I decided it would be fun to have three baddies, rather than just one."

When the Baddies fail in their quest, the little girl kindly gives her hanky to the mouse and her babies to help keep them warm, and that was the original end of the story. However, Julia felt the need to remove the Baddies from the neighbourhood, so an extra double page was added, showing them packing up and going to stay with a new character – a nasty ogre.

There were lots of discussions with Axel about how each of the Baddies should look. They needed to look bad and yet not too terrifying! The ghost was a tricky character because most ghosts in books and films look rather like white sheets. Axel decided that his ghost would look more like a person, as he didn't feel he could get enough expression into a white sheet. He first drew him with an old-fashioned wig but soon dropped that idea.

In this sketch, Axel tries out the top hat look for the first time.

Axel painted a couple of images of the ghost in his old-fashioned wig before switching to the top hat.

Axel Says . . .

"I wanted the ghost to look like a proper villain, but the editor thought he looked too much like a judge with his wig. In the end, I gave him a top hat to look like a Victorian person."

Axel's first witch didn't have a black pointed hat but simply wore a brown scarf. Eventually it was decided that a traditional pointed hat would make her look more witch-like.

In the beginning, the troll was perhaps more like an animal than a fairy-tale character, so Axel gave him a more upright pose.

In the end Axel thought the troll looked a little like a green Gruffalo – a very familiar baddie!

In the original text Julia had written that the Baddies all had runny noses, but it was felt it might be visually unappealing to have dripping noses on every spread, so she reworked the text to take this out.

Bright and inviting, sparkling and blue!
Into the water dived Jonty Gentoo.

Jonty Gentoo

Jonty, the little gentoo penguin, longs to find his true home at the South Pole. One night, he sneaks out of the zoo where he lives with his aunts and sets off on an amazing adventure, all the way to Antarctica (with an accidental detour to the North Pole!).

The original 2024 hardback cover of *Jonty Gentoo: The Adventures of a Penguin*.

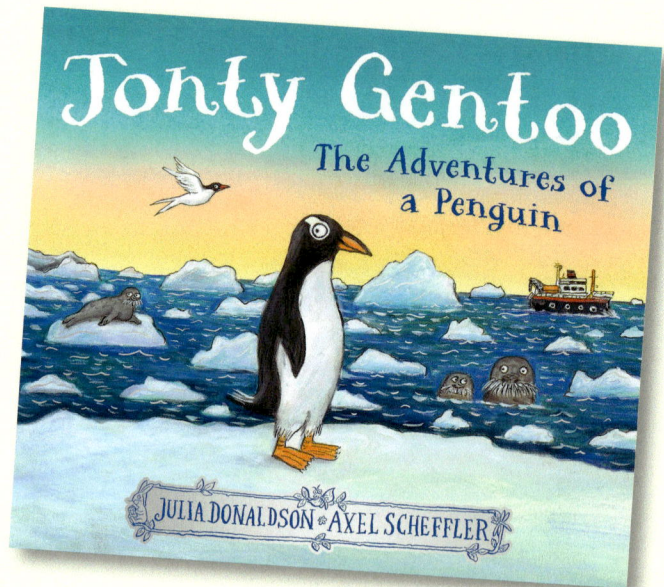

Julia had been planning to write a penguin story for years before she finally produced *Jonty Gentoo*. Her original idea had been that a polar bear at the North Pole and a penguin at the South Pole should be pen friends. When she discovered that there was a bird called an arctic tern which actually flew from pole to pole every year, she decided that a tern could be the messenger between the two characters.

Julia even had a title in mind – *Turn, Tern, Tern* – but she could never work out in her head what the messages between the penguin and the bear would be or how the story would develop. Finally, she abandoned the pen friend idea (who knows, this could be saved for another future book!) and made the penguin the hero of her story, giving the bear and the tern smaller roles.

There are lots of different kinds of penguins – eighteen species, in fact. Julia would have quite liked the book to be about an Adélie penguin, because Axel's daughter is called Adélie so she thought the idea would tickle him. But it would have been hard to find any words to rhyme with Adélie, so she decided instead on a gentoo penguin. The word 'gentoo' has plenty of rhymes, and Julia managed to fit fourteen of them into her story.

At first, Julia wanted the penguin to be a girl, as she felt she already had such a lot of male heroes in her books. But the name had to be right and, although she could have plumped for Jenny or Jeanie Gentoo, Jonty Gentoo sounded a lot better, so the penguin became a boy and now Julia can't imagine him any other way.

As part of her writing process, Julia made a big list of lots of words which rhyme with 'Gentoo' to help her come up with rhymes for the story.

Gentoo, zoo, true, through, blue, view, shoo!, knew, you, blew, crew, queue, how-do-you-do, flew, ooh !

boo, coo, do, dew, few, phew, flu, goo, glue, grew, who, boohoo, loo, moo, mew, new, knew, poo, queue, kangaroo, cockatoo, chew, shoo, shoe, the, too, two, view, toowhit-toowhoo, blue, blew, brew, clue, crew, chew, through, skew, screw, stew, strew, shrew.

Although gentoo penguins are the world's fastest swimming birds, a real-life penguin couldn't swim the huge distances that Jonty does! However, the book is loosely based on real polar creatures and their behaviour. Julia and the publisher decided to include a spread of bird facts at the end of the book called 'Amazing Birds' which tells young readers all about arctic terns and gentoo penguins.

Jonty Gentoo was one of the rare occasions where the character didn't change much from Axel's early drawings. Gentoo penguins have very specific markings: the bonnet-like white stripe on their heads and around their eyes, orange beaks and feet, and orange on the underside of their wings. Axel used reference photos to make sure he captured these key characteristics when developing the character of Jonty Gentoo.

Axel Says . . .

"Everyone loves penguins and I hope that everyone loves Jonty too. I'd also like this book to raise awareness of the threat from climate change to penguins in the wild."

Reference photos such as this one are useful when illustrating real-life animals.

Axel's early character sketches of Jonty Gentoo.

In this first scene from the story, we are introduced to Jonty Gentoo and his family in their home at the zoo.

As usual, Axel did some rough pencil sketches of each page, and sometimes made changes when doing the final artwork.

Axel's rough sketch for this spread focuses on feeding time for the hungry penguins.

The final illustrations feature a bigger scene showing Jonty setting off on his adventure.

Tales from Acorn Wood

In addition to Julia and Axel's picture books, they have also collaborated on a series of simpler lift-the-flap stories for younger children, set in Acorn Wood. Each one is about a different animal and covers an aspect of their daily life, with subjects familiar to toddlers such as playing hide-and-seek, getting dressed, posting letters and baking a birthday cake. The rhyming texts are short, and of course the flaps are fun to lift, even for children too young to follow the stories.

The project started around the time *The Gruffalo* came out. In that story, Axel had been discouraged from dressing the animal characters, but he still enjoyed drawing animals with clothes on, so now Julia was approached by the publisher to write four rhyming stories about animals who would not only wear clothes, but would live in little houses with furniture, like humans.

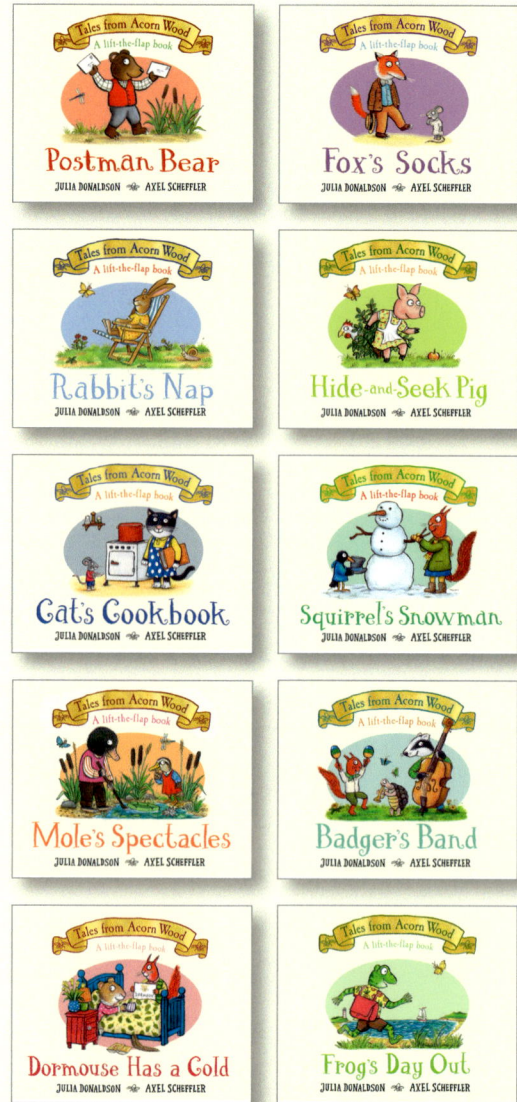

The current editions of the Tales from Acorn Wood series, 2020–2024, Macmillan Children's Books.

The rhyming came easily to Julia, but the big challenge was making sure that each story could have a flap on every double page. She found herself thinking about flaps everywhere she went: a cupboard door, a fridge, a picnic basket, a tent, a toilet seat (or maybe not!).

The first four stories were published in 2000, the same year as *Monkey Puzzle* came out. They were *Postman Bear*, *Fox's Socks*, *Rabbit's Nap* and *Hide-and-Seek Pig*.

At that time, Julia felt she had run out of ideas for flaps, but over twenty years later, she suddenly felt inspired again and came up with four more stories: *Cat's Cookbook*, *Squirrel's Snowman*, *Mole's Spectacles* and *Badger's Band*. More titles followed, with *Dormouse Has a Cold* and *Frog's Day Out*.

Acorn Wood – a name that had been dreamed up by the publisher as a series title for the first four books – becomes a much clearer setting in these later books, with Cat visiting Acorn Library and Dormouse visiting Acorn Fair. There is a real sense of community and friendship, with already familiar characters reappearing in the different stories.

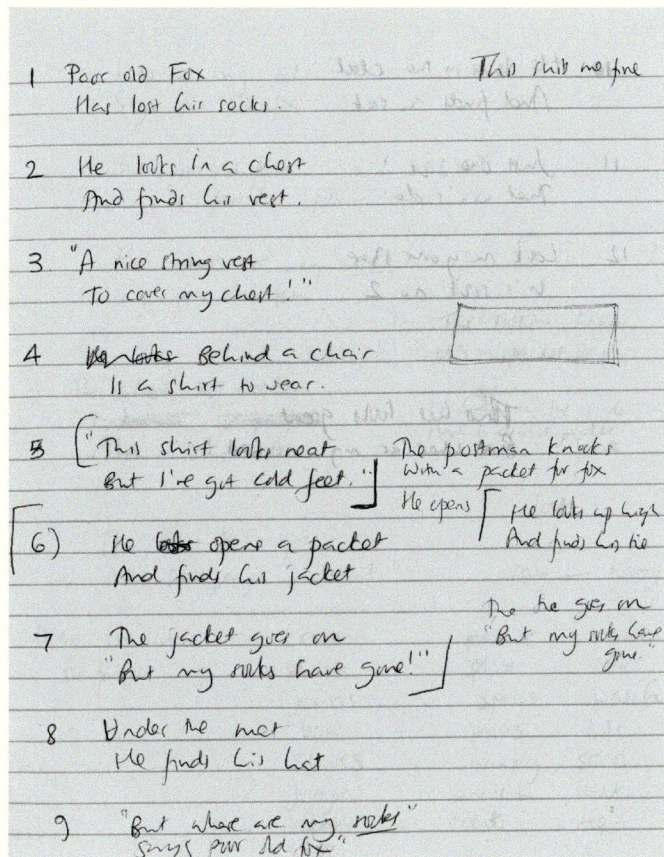

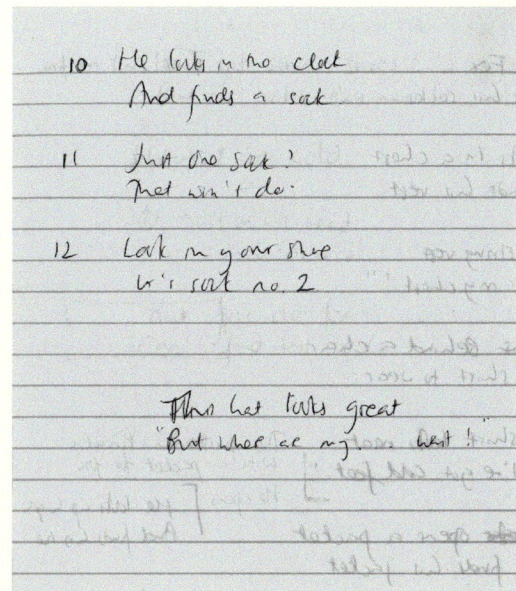

In this early version of *Fox's Socks* from Julia's notebooks, Fox was going to find his jacket inside a packet!

Like Julia, Axel spent a lot of time thinking about the flaps in the books and how they would work. On every spread, the characters interact with an object that becomes a flap for the reader to lift. In *Fox's Socks*, this is Fox searching the house for his missing socks, and in another of the stories, *Cat's Cookbook*, Cat looks through lots of different books at the library for the perfect recipe.

In this early sketch from *Cat's Cookbook*, Axel is worried the book flap might be too small . . .

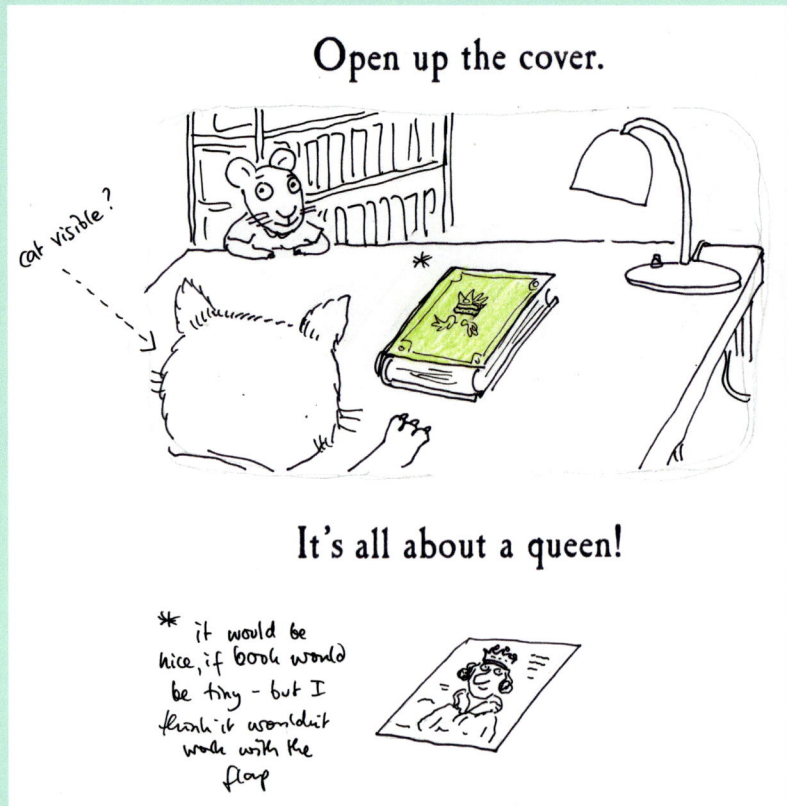

Open up the cover.

cat visible?

It's all about a queen!

* it would be nice, if book would be tiny – but I think it wouldn't work with the flap

Axel's early sketches are also a good opportunity for him to try out different clothing and outfits for the characters. In this colour sketch from *Badger's Band*, Pig looks very different indeed. It was eventually decided that he should look a little bit smarter and more dressed up if he was going to play in a special concert, so Axel gave him a smart button-down shirt and braces, instead of his more casual look!

A rough sketch of this scene where Sheep is introduced shows that other characters had outfit changes too, including the lead character, Badger.

Axel Says . . .

"I like the world of Acorn Wood — little animals wearing clothes, living in their own little world!"

The world of Acorn Wood may seem gorgeously simple, with the animal characters living in burrows and cottages, but if you look closer, Axel brings so much detail and humour in his illustrations.

Axel enjoys adding family portraits inside each of the character's homes, such as this photo on Bear's writing desk in *Postman Bear*.

Squirrel's bed frame in *Squirrel's Snowman* has little acorn and leaf details as a nod to the woodland setting.

Other Work
and Partnerships

Find out all about Julia and Axel's other work and
interests, and the adaptation of their much-loved
picture books to stage, screen and beyond.

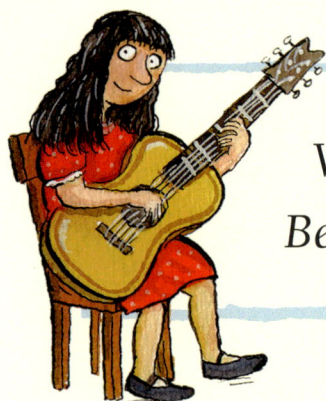

Why are your stories so often in rhyme?
Because I wrote songs for a very long time.

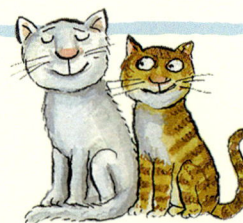

Music and Song

Julia had been a songwriter long before she wrote any books, so it was natural that, once the books started appearing, she would write songs to go with them. She often performs these songs at her live shows, accompanied by Malcolm on guitar.

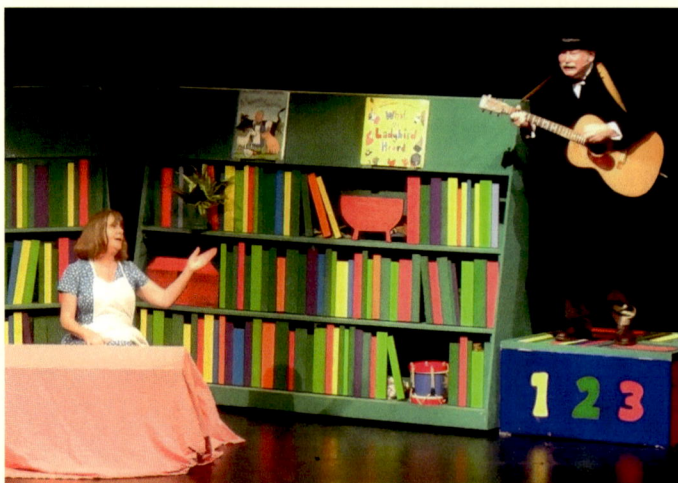

Julia and Malcolm performing the *A Squash and a Squeeze* song. Julia is playing the part of the little old lady, and Malcolm is the wise old man.

Many of Julia's picture-book songs have been recorded, sung by well-known actors, including Imelda Staunton, Josie Lawrence and Jim Carter. These recordings are available to listen to alongside the audiobook recordings of the stories.

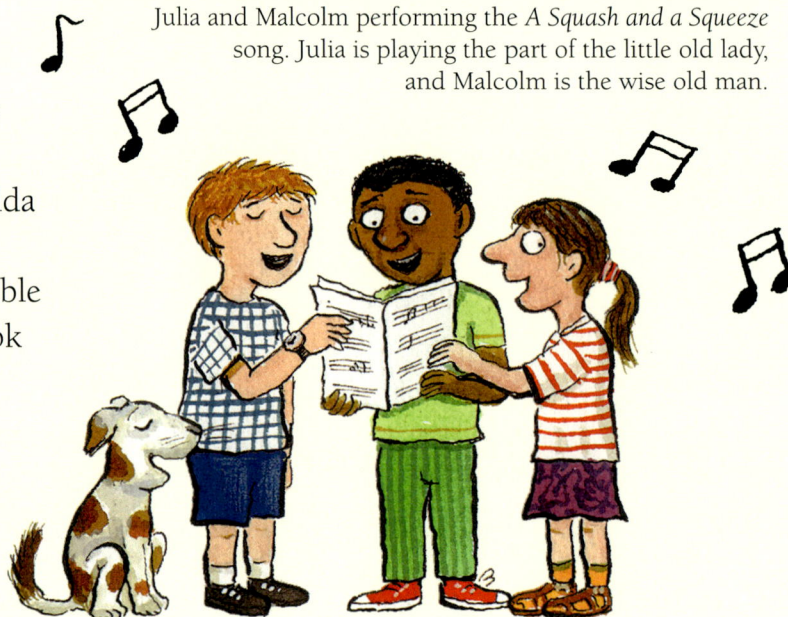

There are also recordings of versions sung by Julia herself, accompanied by live musicians. In 2022, Julia and Malcolm spent a number of days at a professional recording studio to record new versions of all of her picture-book stories and songs. They were joined by a live band – including Malcolm on the guitar, of course – who recorded instrumental accompaniments for all of the songs.

Julia hard at work in the recording studio.

Axel has done lovely illustrations for these song books, including this moustachioed hare jumping over the back of the tortoise!

The words, and in some cases, the musical scores of these picture-book songs can be found in a range of special songbooks, along with some of Julia's action songs and others based on familiar Aesop's fables such as 'The Hare and the Tortoise'.

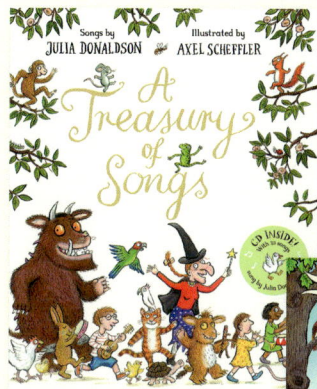

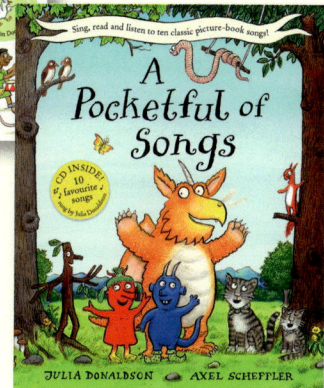

Two gift collections of Julia's picture-book songs, illustrated by Axel – *A Treasury of Songs*, Macmillan Children's Books, 2016; *A Pocketful of Songs*, Alison Green Books, 2022.

Poetry and Plays

Julia has always had a passion for poetry. As a child, she wanted to be a poet, and learned verses from her favourite poetry book to recite. All but one of her books with Axel are written in verse, and so are over forty of the other books she has written. Julia has also written many poems, some of which are published in *Crazy Mayonnaisy Mum*, illustrated by Nick Sharratt.

Julia reciting a verse at a school nativity play.

Poems to Perform, Macmillan Children's Books, 2013.
Rock-a-bye Rumpus, Macmillan Children's Books, 2022.
Pick and Mix Poetry, Macmillan Children's Books, 2024.

She has also curated a collection called *Pick and Mix Poetry,* which includes over 300 poems for children, from unforgettable classics to contemporary works from around the world. Fully illustrated by Becky Thorns, this book was a real labour of love for Julia, who hopes it will spark a life-long love of poetry for many children.

During her time as the Children's Laureate, Julia produced a collection called *Poems to Perform*, which includes some of her favourite poets, such as Eleanor Farjeon and Michael Rosen. All the poems in this anthology can be read aloud or acted out by two or more voices.

For younger children, Julia has compiled a collection of action rhymes, *Rock-a-bye Rumpus*, with pictures by Sébastien Braun. It includes traditional verses, poems by other poets, and a few by Julia herself. Julia and Malcolm had fun recording these poems with four of their grandchildren for the audio which accompanies the book.

Three of Julia's grandchildren rehearsing for the audio recording of *Rock-a-bye Rumpus*.

Julia has loved plays ever since she trod the boards as a fairy in *A Midsummer Night's Dream* at the age of twelve. It was a magical experience that she has never forgotten.

She first started writing short plays for reading groups when she was helping at her eldest son's primary school. The children loved reading all the different parts and Julia saw that it was a great way of improving their reading skills and their confidence. She has since written very many such short plays for educational publishers, and is particularly proud of a series called Plays to Read: forty-eight short plays, each with six characters, written by herself and other authors whom she commissioned.

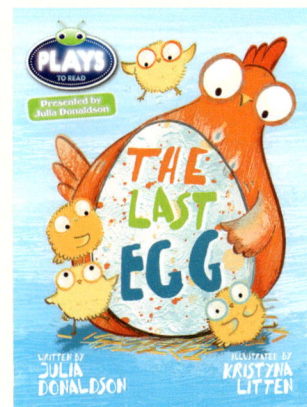

The Last Egg, Pearson 2013

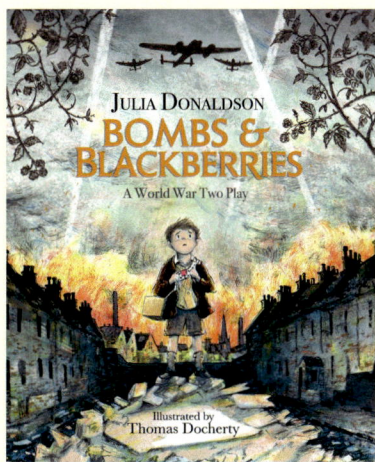

Bombs and Blackberries, Hodder Children's Books, 2020.

The first play that Julia wrote for a whole class was *Persephone*, based on the Greek myth about a goddess's daughter who is captured by the King of the Underworld. This has now been published and is often performed by primary school children, along with two of her other plays for a whole class: *Bombs and Blackberries*, about children evacuated during World War Two; and *Chariots and Champions*, set in Roman Britain.

Julia has visited schools all over the world and she likes to encourage the children to act out her stories. Seeing how much children enjoy and benefit from this experience, she has now adapted some of her picture books into plays, and has also created a series called Plays to Act. Each of these is designed for a whole class and based on a well-known picture book, some by herself and some by other authors.

Tyrannosaurus Drip: A Play, Pearson, 2013.
The Gruffalo Play, Macmillan Children's Books, 2014.

What a Performance!

With experience busking, acting, song-writing and singing, there is no doubt that Julia is a born performer. When she isn't at her writing desk, Julia enjoys visiting festivals and performing in her own shows. She has a unique energy and ability to connect with her audience, and children love watching the storytelling – and sometimes coming on stage to take part.

Julia playing the witch from *Room on the Broom* in her show, *The Gruffalo, the Witch and the Warthog* at Edinburgh Fringe Festival.

Julia Says . . .

"I really enjoy getting children in the audience to help me act out the stories and join in with the songs."

Malcolm usually accompanies Julia, playing guitar and acting characters from a fox to a troll! He often jokes that he only gets the parts of stupid or nasty characters, but Julia knows that he secretly enjoys playing the villains. Other members of Julia's family get involved too, including her sister Mary, and her sons, Alastair and Jerry.

Julia is the mouse, Julia's sister Mary the owl, James Huntingdon the snake and Malcolm the sly Fox in a performance of *The Gruffalo*.

Many props and costumes are needed to bring the stories to life. Julia has a dedicated 'props room' in her house, which is packed full of puppets, masks and outfits which she uses for her shows – everything from the head of the Highway Rat to the ears of the Mouse. Some of Julia's props can be seen in the portrait of her which hangs in the National Portrait Gallery in London.

Julia's 'props room'.

Painted by the artist Peter Monkman.

Julia and Axel on the *Tiddler* promotional tour in Germany.

Occasionally, Axel joins in the acting fun, his star roles being the wise old man in *A Squash and a Squeeze*, and the Owl in *The Gruffalo*. Together, Julia and Axel have toured Germany several times and acted out their stories in Axel's native language, German. However, he is better known for entertaining through drawing workshops in which children can watch him draw his characters and even have a go themselves.

The Stage Shows

From the West End in London to Broadway in New York, there are many wonderful theatre productions of Julia and Axel's books which return to the stage year after year. *The Gruffalo* was the first of their books to be adapted for the theatre in 2001 by touring theatre company, Tall Stories.

It received glowing reviews and has gone on to entertain audiences across the UK, Europe, North America, Asia and Australia.

Actors playing the Gruffalo and the Mouse from *The Gruffalo* stage show, by Tall Stories.

A scene from *The Snail and the Whale*.

Tall Stories have also adapted a number of Julia and Axel's other picture-book stories: *The Gruffalo's Child*, *Room on the Broom*, *The Smeds and the Smoos* and *The Snail and the Whale*. They added two extra characters to the play of *The Snail and the Whale*, an adventurous young girl and her sailor father, who tell the story of the tiny snail and the great big whale to the accompaniment of an electric viola.

The Gruffalo has been adapted for many settings, but in January 2019 there was a Gruffalo first – it became an opera! *The Gruffalo Opera* was performed in Berlin, Germany, and both Julia and Axel attended a performance. Staged by conductor and composer Iván Fischer, it featured five opera singers as well as instruments to represent each of the characters, against a background of Axel's illustrations.

A scene from *The Gruffalo Opera*.

Other companies have adapted Julia and Axel's works too. London's Little Angel Theatre put on *The Smartest Giant in Town*, using clever puppetry and live music.

George the giant with his new friends, the mice.

Freckle Productions have also staged adaptations of Julia and Axel's books, including *Zog* and *Stick Man*, with songs specially written for each show.

They have also put together a show called *Tiddler and Other Terrific Tales*, which cleverly weaves a selection of stories together: *Tiddler*, *Monkey Puzzle*, *The Smartest Giant in Town* and *A Squash and a Squeeze*.

A scene from *Tiddler*.

Watching one of these family shows is often the first time that a child will experience live theatre, and it is a very special moment – as well as lots of fun!

A scene from *Zog*.

Amazing Animations

The wizardry of computer animation has now brought *The Gruffalo* and other Julia and Axel picture books to life on screen. Since 2008, the animation company Magic Light Pictures has produced a number of acclaimed thirty-minute films of their books, from *Stick Man* to *Superworm*. These stunning films have won more than forty awards between them, including two BAFTAs. The BBC showings have become a family fixture on Christmas Day in the UK, watched by an excited audience of millions every year.

The little Mouse and his scary companion, the Gruffalo, brought to life in the film adaptation.

Taking a much-loved story and adapting it for the screen is a complex creative process. A huge team of people is involved: producers, directors, animators, musicians and voice actors. To turn a thirty-two page book into a thirty-minute film, the screenwriters use their skills to expand and add to the original story. The final script is designed as a storyboard – a set of rough pictures that shows every stage of the film from beginning to end.

For *The Gruffalo*, *The Gruffalo's Child* and *Room on the Broom*, Magic Light Pictures used CGI – computer-generated imagery – against a background of three-dimensional 'real-life' sets built by set designers in a studio. The moving characters were then skillfully created on computer, staying as close to Axel's vision as possible. For the later films, from *Stick Man* onwards, the films were made entirely using CGI.

Each film has its own original musical score and a cast of well-known actors voicing the characters, with famous actors including Helena Bonham Carter, Rob Brydon and James Corden bringing them to life.

(Above) Zog and his school friends practising their flying tricks with Madam Dragon.
(Right) The Snail and the Whale on an adventure around the world.
(Below) The Smeds and the Smoos living happily together on a distant planet.

Julia and Axel chose to work with Magic Light Pictures because they trusted them to keep to the spirit of their original stories, while bringing another dimension to their work. The result is a visual treat: stunning animations that have become classics in their own right.

The World Beyond the Books

The worlds of Julia and Axel's stories are not confined to the page, stage and screen, however. When they first created the Gruffalo more than twenty-five years ago, they could not have imagined that their wart-nosed monster would one day be everywhere – from toys and stationery to clothes, food and even shampoo! And it isn't just the Gruffalo; there is also plenty of merchandise for other popular characters such as Zog and Stick Man.

There are also numerous opportunities to take a sneak peek inside the world of all of Julia and Axel's picture books. In 2018/19, an exhibition at Discover Children's Story Centre in London, UK, transformed scenes from twelve of their books into wonderful immersive worlds. Visitors could enter Charlie Cook's cosy sitting room, explore the deep dark wood with the Gruffalo and have an underwater adventure with Tiddler. The exhibition, called 'A World Inside a Book – The Gruffalo, Dragons and other Creatures' was inspired by the idea of 'worlds within books' from *Charlie Cook's Favourite Book*.

Julia and Axel reading in Charlie Cook's cosy armchair. Julia even used some of the leftover fabric to make blinds and a tablecloth for her study at home!

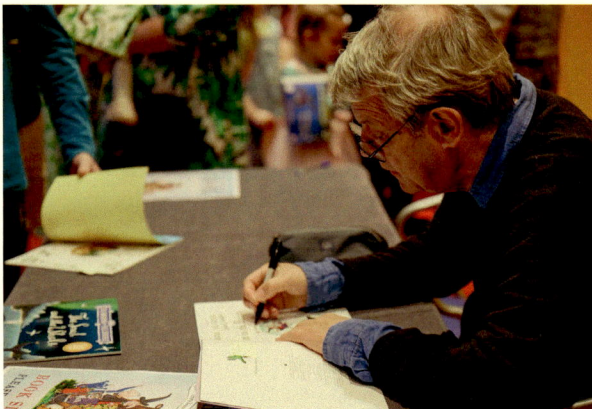

Axel enjoyed visiting the Lowry and signing books for visitors.

In 2023, the Lowry arts centre near Manchester, UK, curated a free exhibition called 'Julia and Axel: Thirty Years of Favourite Stories'. With family-focused fun, including story writing, drawing, dress-up and play, as well as a peek behind the scenes at Julia and Axel's creative process, the exhibition aimed to inspire future creativity and welcomed over 100,000 visitors between July and December 2023.

Take a Trail

There are also a number of interactive adventures and experiences based on the much-loved stories. The Forestry Commission has created trails in deep dark woods across the UK, where children can roam outdoors, take part in fun activities and try to spot the giant statues of characters from *The Gruffalo* along the way. These proved so popular that they have created other family trails all based on Julia and Axel's books; you can now help the lost Stick Man to find his family tree, learn about flying creatures with Zog, and investigate the world of mini-beasts with the mighty Superworm – all while taking a walk in the woods.

In 2017, children's theme park, Chessington World of Adventures in Surrey, UK, created a brand new water ride based on *The Gruffalo*. Riders join Mouse on a river boat journey through the deep dark wood, with exciting twists and turns along the way. They have since created a *Room on the Broom* magical broomstick experience, too. There is also lots of interactive fun to be had at locations around the country: The Gruffalo and Friends Clubhouse in Blackpool has a Deep Dark Wood soft play, Zog Dragon School Challenge, themed café and more; and Warwick Castle has a range of activities based on *Zog*, including an adventure playground, activity trail and live shows.

A Royal Replica

In 2024, visitors to Windsor Castle were treated to a very special exhibition created to celebrate the centenary of Queen Mary's Dolls' House. The dolls' house was first completed in 1924 for Queen Mary, consort of King George V, and included a library with hundreds of miniature books, many written by well-known authors of the day. For the anniversary celebrations, twenty-one new miniature books were created and Julia and Axel were honoured to be asked to contribute a tiny version of *The Gruffalo,* which is handwritten by Julia and includes unique, new illustrations by Axel.

Some pages from the Queen Mary's Dolls' House mini-book of *The Gruffalo*. Axel imagined brand new images for this special occasion, including some delicious Gruffalo crumble!

Becoming Children's Laureate

Julia and Axel have received many prizes and honours for their work over the years, both together and individually.

It was a huge honour for Julia when she was asked to be the UK Children's Laureate in 2011. The role is awarded every two years to a children's writer or illustrator in celebration of their outstanding achievements. Being Laureate gave Julia the chance to promote three things which are very dear to her: performance, libraries and stories for deaf children.

In 2012, Julia went on a six-week tour of British libraries, which began at John O'Groats in Scotland and finished 1,407 kilometres away at Land's End in the south-west of England. The children who came along were asked to present a story, song or poem, and Julia did the same – a wonderful opportunity for everyone to enjoy performing.

At a time when many libraries are being closed and their budgets cut, Julia used her time in the spotlight to speak with politicians and to write passionately about the positive effects that libraries have on children.

Julia posing in front of the famous signpost in John O'Groats.

Julia also came up with a new poem called 'The Library Rap', written especially for National Libraries Day.

Everyone is welcome to walk through the door.
It really doesn't matter if you're rich or poor.
There are books in boxes and books on shelves.
They're free for you to borrow, so help yourselves.

– The first verse of 'The Library Rap'

A Prince and a Hat

In 2019, Julia was invited to Buckingham Palace to meet Prince William and receive a CBE for her Services to Literature. It was a very special moment, made even more memorable when Julia's hat fell off during her presentation, bringing a smile to the Prince's face. When the press saw what happened, they immediately made the connection between Julia and the witch who loses her hat in *Room on the Broom*. Julia dedicated her CBE to all those who work in the world of children's books.

Julia with her sons, Jerry and Alastair, outside Buckingham Palace.

A Magical World

In 2020 the BBC released a documentary, *The Magical World of Julia Donaldson*, celebrating her life and work, with contributions from well-known fans including Michael Rosen and Victoria Coren Mitchell.

A Masterclass

Julia introducing her BBC Maestro course.

Julia is so well-respected as an author that many aspiring writers would love to learn from her. To help them, she has filmed an online course of twenty-four lessons about how to write children's picture books. The course is part of a subscription service called BBC Maestro. Julia talks about every aspect of picture books, including ideas, plot development, characters and rhyme. She also introduces some other experts, including her editor, her agent and, of course, Axel, who all participate in some of the lessons and give their tips.

Illustrator of the Year

Axel's shelves are heaped with prizes and he has received many accolades as an illustrator during his career. He has been awarded multiple Nielsen Platinum Bestseller Awards, for selling over one million copies of several of his books.

Axel receiving Platinum Bestseller Awards for
The Gruffalo and *The Gruffalo's Child*.

In 2018, Axel received a very special prize at the British Book Awards – also known as the 'Nibbies' because winners receive a large golden pen nib. He was chosen to be the first ever recipient of their Illustrator of the Year Award for all his incredible work on so many books.

Axel is often asked to judge awards and competitions for illustrators. He has previously been a judge for competitions such as the Macmillan Prize for Illustration which awards students at art schools around the UK, and Oscar's Book Prize which celebrates the best book for children under five. He has also been on the panel for the Association of Illustrators' World Illustration Awards which celebrates outstanding work by artists around the world.

In 2022, Axel was honoured to be awarded the Cross of the Order of Merit of the Federal Republic of Germany (*Bundesverdienstkreuz*).

Axel in the Post

In 2006, Axel was asked to design the official Christmas card for the Treasury by the Chancellor at that time, Gordon Brown. Axel's colourful card featured happy children reading around a Christmas tree, with a ministerial red box in the corner to represent the Treasury. The scene is his take on the annual children's Christmas party at No. 11 Downing Street, which in 2006 was hosted by the literacy charity BookTrust.

Another Christmas treat followed in 2012 when the Royal Mail commissioned Axel to illustrate the official Christmas stamps for that year.

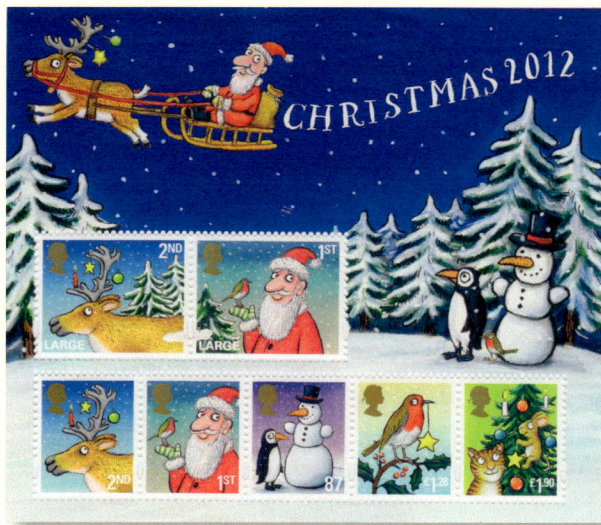

Axel's work adorned envelopes across the nation for a second time when the 20th anniversary of *The Gruffalo* was celebrated in 2019. The Royal Mail commissioned six special-edition Gruffalo stamps to mark the occasion. In Germany, a special Gruffalo stamp was also issued to celebrate Axel's work.

Axel's Envelopes

Wouldn't it be nice to wake up one morning and receive a letter inside a hand-painted envelope that was made especially for you? That's what many of Axel's friends and work colleagues have discovered in their post. If you're lucky enough to know Axel well, you might get an envelope with an animal, a person, or an object that is special to you, painted on the front and back. Julia, of course, has been one of the lucky recipients.

Over his long career Axel has created so many of these fantastic envelopes that, in 2022, two exhibitions were held in Germany. Axel Scheffler's Fantastical Letter Illustrations displayed two hundred of Axel's stunning envelopes, showing a huge variety of animals, people, fantastical creatures – and, of course, Gruffalos! A book was later published to collect all these unique illustrations together called *A Friendship in Correspondence*.

Julia Says . . .

"Axel started sending letters and postcards – he still does – and he would decorate the envelopes, sometimes cleverly incorporating the stamp."

Here are some of the colourful envelopes Axel has sent to his friends and colleagues over the years.

A Force for Good

Julia and Axel have tried to make use of the much-loved characters from their books to help people in difficult times. When the Covid-19 crisis hit the world in 2020, many countries went into lockdown. Families everywhere were trying to cope with the new rules and children suffered from not being able to attend school. Julia and Axel put their heads together to think of a way to help children understand what was happening. Axel came up with a brilliant idea to show characters from their picture books coping with social distancing, home schooling and lockdown life in general. Axel re-drew popular characters such as the Gruffalo, the Smartest Giant and Stick Man, while Julia wrote light-hearted rhyming couplets to accompany the images.

Look me up and down,
I'm the cleanest giant in town!

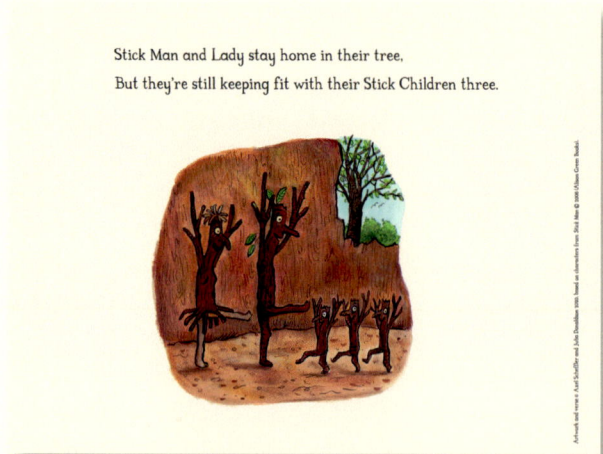

Stick Man and Lady stay home in their tree,
But they're still keeping fit with their Stick Children three.

Two of the twelve images published in *The Guardian* newspaper.

Julia also produced a weekly online broadcast called "Julia Donaldson and Friends" to entertain children at home during lockdown. Every week, Julia and Malcolm would act out one of her songs or stories, followed by Axel or one of her other illustrators (in their own homes) drawing a character from the books. You can still access these videos on Julia's website.

Axel draws in twelve of the episodes, including the final broadcast, in which Julia and Malcolm venture into their local deep dark wood to act out *The Gruffalo*, while Axel, in his garden, shows everyone how to draw a gruffalo and a mouse.

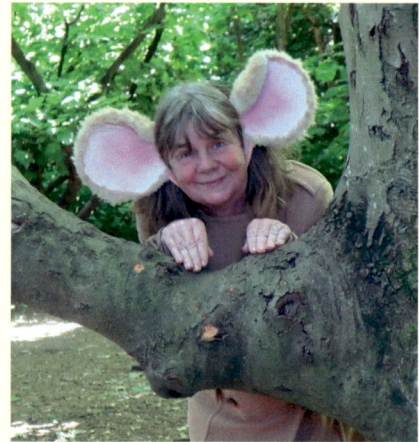

Julia exploring her local deep dark wood as the Mouse in one of her Julia Donaldson and Friends broadcasts.

Axel was also very proud to have illustrated a book for young children teaching them about the pandemic. It was originally released as a free digital book for primary school age children, and was later released as a physical book with a proportion of each sale going to NHS Charities Together.

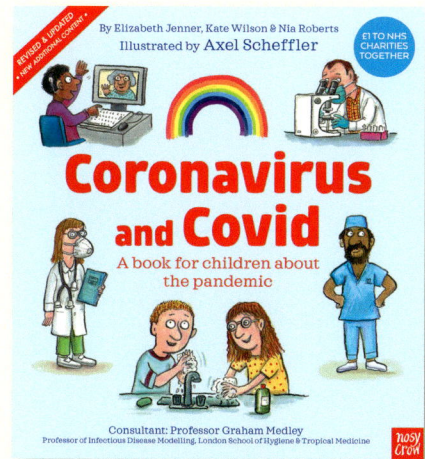

Coronavirus and Covid, Nosy Crow, 2021.

Julia joined Axel on a march to protest against the UK leaving the EU. *The Gruffalo* is an Anglo-German creation and would never have existed without free movement of people within the EU.

This was not the first time Axel has used his illustrations to draw attention to current events. On 23 June 2016, the United Kingdom voted to leave the European Union. This was a very sad day for Axel as an EU citizen living in the UK. During the build-up to the vote, Axel had illustrations published in multiple newspapers in the UK and Germany to show his concerns about the future.

Axel later asked other illustrators to join him in creating an exhibition celebrating their love for Europe. A book of the exhibition, called *Drawing Europe Together*, was published in November 2018. Forty-five artists who live and work in different parts of Europe drew or painted their vision of Europe and what it has meant to them. There were contributions from many famous illustrators, such as Judith Kerr, Quentin Blake and Chris Riddell.

Axel's proposal for a European Heraldic Animal, the EU-le (a play on the German word for owl, 'eule').

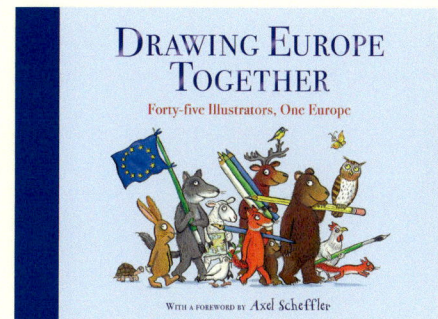

Drawing Europe Together, Macmillan Children's Books, 2018.

Charities and Patronage

Axel is patron of Three Peas, a charity that helps people forced to flee their homes in war-torn countries. Three Peas has established strong partnerships on the ground in refugee camps in northern Greece and on the islands of Chios, Lesbos and Samos. They provide emergency support and also run and support long-term projects. Axel has donated many of his sketches and artworks to be auctioned for them, including illustrations of the Gruffalo.

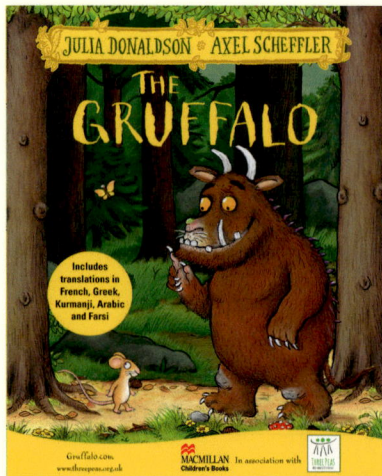

In 2022, a special multi-language edition of *The Gruffalo* was created, in collaboration with the charity, to be distributed to refugee camps for use in libraries, community centres and schools. This special edition of the book includes the English language story as well as translations in five languages: French, Greek, Kurmanji, Arabic and Farsi.

Axel headed up a fundraising book called *Kind*, written by Alison Green, in conjunction with thirty-seven other illustrators. The book explores the many ways children can be kind, from sharing their toys and games to helping those from other countries feel welcome. All proceeds from each book go to the Three Peas charity.

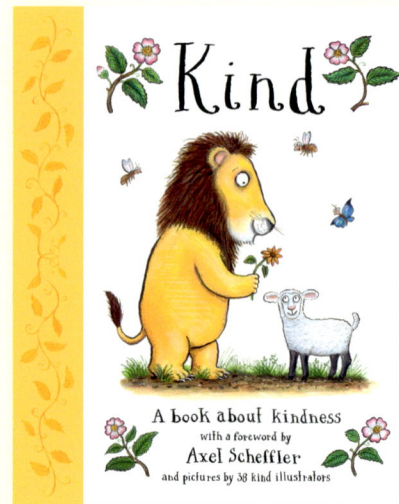

Axel has also used his illustrating talents to help raise funds for refugees escaping the war in Ukraine. In March 2022, he painted a special *Room on the Broom* witch. Entitled Peace Witch, she was dressed in Ukrainian flag colours. The witch was sold at auction and the proceeds went to the charity Book Aid for Ukraine.

Julia is also patron of several charities, including Storybook Dads, which enables prisoners to read bedtime stories to their children; Amaze, which supports carers of young people with special needs and disabilities; Read for Good which brings stories to children in hospital; and Action for Deafness, which provides support for those with hearing loss.

Julia herself wears hearing aids and, when she was the Children's Laureate, she helped a group of deaf students write a book about sign language called *What the Jackdaw Saw*, which was then published with illustrations by Nick Sharratt. She also wrote *Freddie and the Fairy*, a story about a deaf fairy and a mumbling boy, which has pictures by Karen George.

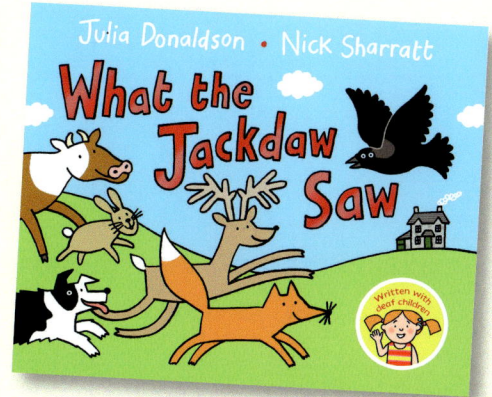

What the Jackdaw Saw, Macmillan Children's Books, 2015.

Julia likes to ensure that her books are as accessible as possible, and she has filmed versions of some of her songs using Makaton. In her shows, she often performs *The Gruffalo* with British Sign Language signs. Many of her and Axel's books are also available as free braille and audio-described versions for blind and partially sighted children through the Living Paintings charity. In these special versions of the books, children can enjoy the illustrations by feeling raised images of the characters.

Early in her career, Julia was a writer in residence at Easterhouse, a disadvantaged area of Glasgow, where she set up and ran an adult writers' group called All Write. The group is still going twenty years later, and has produced several anthologies of their work.

Julia is also a patron for the children's hospice, Chestnut Tree House, and during her visits there the children's families take part in her storytelling sessions.

Conclusion

Julia Donaldson and Axel Scheffler have been creating some of the world's best-loved children's books for over thirty years. Starting with their very first picture book, *A Squash and a Squeeze* in 1993, they have introduced readers to countless imaginary worlds and characters, from dragons to witches, tiny minibeasts to kind-hearted giants – and, of course, everyone's favourite monster, the Gruffalo.

The winning combination of Julia's rhythmical read-aloud texts with Axel's warm and witty illustrations has charmed generations of readers. Their brilliant characters and vibrant worlds have also taken on a life off the page, inspiring award-winning stage shows, exhibitions, films and more, and firmly establishing them as the world's favourite picture-book partnership.

With millions of copies of their books sold in over 100 languages and dialects, Julia and Axel's stories continue to delight children around the world, with an appeal that is sure to endure for years to come.

The publisher would like to thank the following for permission to reproduce copyright material:

p.17 top right, GRANGER – Historical Picture Archive / Alamy Stock Photo, bottom left, Cover artwork by Charlotte Voake from *The Further Adventures of the Owl and the Pussy-cat* by Julia Donaldson, published by Puffin. Cover reprinted by permission of Penguin Books Limited; **p.21** top right, *The Spaghetti Song*, copyright © 2020, Edizioni El, Trieste, Italy; **p.25** *Petzi* copyright © 2024 Rasmus Klump P/S; **p.27** *Papa Schnapp* by Tomi Ungerer, published by Diogenes Verlag, Zurich, 1987. First published as *I Am Papa Snap* and *These Are My Favourite No Such Stories* by Harper and Row, New York, 1971; **p.32** top left, Cover image courtesy of The Resurgence Trust www.resurgence.org, bottom, *The Piemakers* by Helen Cresswell. Cover reprinted by permission of Faber and Faber Ltd.; **p.33** top, *Die Geschichte von vier Kindern, die um die Welt segelten* by Edward Lear and Axel Scheffler. © 1991 Beltz & Gelberg in der Verlagsgruppe Beltz, Weinheim Basel, middle, *You're a Hero, Daley B!* Written by Jon Blake and illustrated by Axel Scheffler. Text © Jon Blake 1994. Illustrations © Axel Scheffler 1994. Reproduced by permission of Walker Books Ltd, London, SE11 5HJ. www.walker.co.uk; **p.37** bottom, Dave Pickthorn © BBC Archive; **p.39** bottom, © Steve Ullathorne; **p.42** bottom, © Mike Lawn/Weekend Magazine; **p.44** top, carstenbrandt / istock; **p.45** middle, © Eliz Hüseyin; **p.81** middle, World History Archive / Alamy Stock Photo; **p.138** middle, bpperry / istock; **p.149** top, *The Last Egg* by Julia Donaldson, illustrated by Kristyna Litten. Cover reproduced with permission of Pearson Education Ltd., middle, *Bombs and Blackberries* by Julia Donaldson, illustrated by Thomas Docherty, published by Hodder Children's Books. Cover reproduced with permission of Hachette Children's Group through PLSclear, bottom, *Tyrannosaurus Drip: A Play* by Julia Donaldson, illustrated by David Roberts. Based on the original picture book published by Macmillan Children's Books. Cover reproduced with permission of Pearson Education Ltd.; **p150** © Steve Ullathorne; **p151** middle, photo by Steve Ullathorne; **p152** top and middle, *The Gruffalo / The Snail and the Whale* © Tobias Dobrzynski, courtesy of Tall Stories, bottom, *The Gruffalo Opera* © Bettina Stöß; **p.153** top, © Ellie Kurttz, courtesy of the Little Angel Theatre, middle, Tiddler © Robin Savage, courtesy of Freckle Productions, bottom, Zog © Mark Senior, courtesy of Freckle Productions; **pp154–155** The Gruffalo © Orange Eyes Ltd. 2009, Zog © Magic Light Pictures Ltd. 2018, The Snail and the Whale © Magic Light Picture Ltd. 2019, The Smeds and the Smoos © Magic Light Pictures Ltd. 2022. Licensed by Magic Light Pictures Ltd.; **p.156** middle, Photo © Debra Hurford Brown, reproduced by permission of Discover Children's Story Centre; **p.157** Image files © Royal Collection Enterprises Limited 2024 | Royal Collection Trust; **p159**. bottom, © BBC Maestro; **p.160** top, © The Bestseller Awards; **p.161** middle, Christmas 2012 stamps © Axel Scheffler 2012, reproduced by permission of Royal Mail, Gruffalo 20th Anniversary stamps © Julia Donaldson and Axel Scheffler 1999, 2019, reproduced by permission of Royal Mail. Licensed by Magic Light Pictures Ltd., bottom, German Gruffalo stamp, designed by Bettina Walter, Bonn. © Julia Donaldson and Axel Scheffler 1999. Licensed by Magic Light Pictures Ltd.; **p.165** top *Coronavirus and Covid*, Text copyright © Elizabeth Jenner, Kate Wilson & Nia Roberts 2020, Illustration copyright © Axel Scheffler 2021, cover reproduced by permission of Nosy Crow Limited; **p.168** © Antonio Olmos/Guardian/eyevine; **p.170** Stick Man © Orange Eyes Ltd. 2015. Licensed by Magic Light Pictures Ltd., Illustrator of the Year award © Ross Maclennan/The Bookseller, *The Magical World of Julia Donaldson* © BBC; **p.171** The Gruffalo (stage show) © Tobias Dobrzynski, courtesy of Tall Stories, The Gruffalo (animation) © Orange Eyes Ltd. Licensed by Magic Light Pictures, Julia Donaldson picture-book writing course © BBC Maestro, Julia and Axel in 2023 © Antonio Olmos/Guardian/eyevine.

Every effort has been made to identify copyright holders and obtain their permission for the use of copyright material. Notification of any additions or corrections that should be incorporated in future reprints or editions of this book would be greatly appreciated.

Timeline

Julia Donaldson and Axel Scheffler have been creating books together since 1993. Join them on their long and successful partnership . . .

1993
The first story written by Julia and illustrated by Axel, *A Squash and a Squeeze*, is published.

1999
The Gruffalo is published – and wins the Nestlé Smarties Prize the same year.

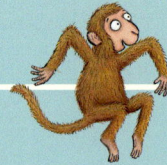

2000
The Gruffalo wins the Blue Peter Award for best book to read aloud. Julia and Axel publish their third joint project, *Monkey Puzzle*, and the first titles in their Tales from Acorn Wood series.

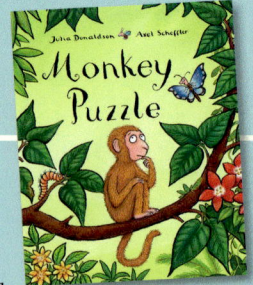

2011
Julia is made UK Children's Laureate – and *The Highway Rat* scurries into bookshops.

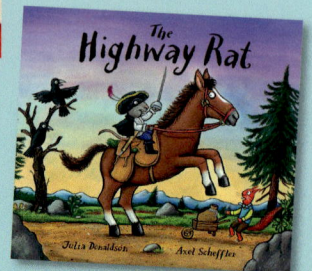

2012
Superworm is published.

2014
Everyone's invited to *The Scarecrow's Wedding*.

2016
Zog returns in *Zog and the Flying Doctors*.

2018
The Ugly Five is published. Axel is awarded the Illustrator of the Year Award at the British Book Awards.

2019
The Smeds and the Smoos arrives, *The Gruffalo Opera* opens in Berlin and Julia is honoured with a CBE.

2020
The BBC releases a documentary about Julia, *The Magical World of Julia Donaldson*.

2001
The Gruffalo stage show premieres and *Room on the Broom* is published.

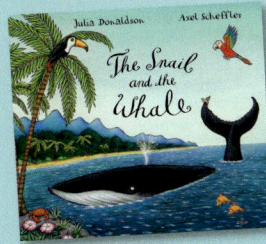

2004
Five years on, *The Gruffalo* gets a sequel, *The Gruffalo's Child*.

2003
. . . and a year after that by *The Snail and the Whale*.

2002
This is followed a year later by *The Smartest Giant in Town* . . .

2005
Charlie Cook's Favourite Book is published.

2010
A new character, *Zog*, makes its first appearance.

2009
Tabby McTat is introduced and *The Gruffalo* animated film premieres on Christmas Day.

2008
. . . and a whole family of sticks arrive in *Stick Man*.

2007
Tiddler makes his first splash . . .

2020
The Gruffalo is now translated into over 100 languages!

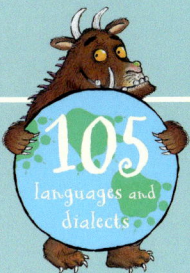

105 languages and dialects

2021
Julia's picture-book writing course launches on BBC Maestro.

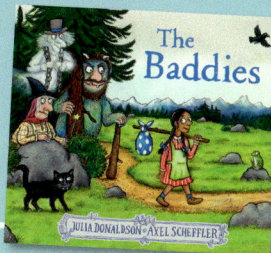

2022
It's time to meet *The Baddies*.

2023
Julia and Axel celebrate a creative partnership that has lasted thirty years.

2024
Julia and Axel reach thirty books together with *Frog's Day Out* and *Jonty Gentoo*.